HeartHealthy Cooking

DELICIOUS EVERYDAY RECIPES

EDITORS

Barbara Ledermann MSC., RD and

Bridget Wilson P.H.EC.

KEY PORTER BOOKS

Canadian Cataloguing in Publication Data

Main entry under title:

Heart healthy cooking : delicious everyday recipes

Includes index.
ISBN 1-55263-294-6

1. Heart – Diseases – Diet therapy – Recipes. I. Ledermann, Barbara A. (Barbara Anne), 1969- . II. Wilson, Bridget.

RC684.D5H433 2000   641.5'6311   C00-931803-8

The publisher gratefully acknowledges the support of the Canada Council for the Arts and the Ontario Arts Council for its publishing program.

We acknowledge the financial support of the Government of Canada through the Book Publishing Industry Development Program (BPIDP) for our publishing activities.

Key Porter Books Limited
70 The Esplanade
Toronto, Ontario
Canada M5E 1R2

www.keyporter.com

Illustration on page 13 is ©Minister of Public Works and Government Services Canada, 1997
Cat. No. H39-252/1992E ISBN 0-662-19648-1
No changes permitted. Reprint permission not required.

Design: Peter Maher
Photography: Pete Paterson
Food styling: Sue Henderson
Prop styling: Catherine MacFadyen

00 01 02 03 6 5 4 3 2 1

Printed in Canada

Acknowledgments

For more than 20 years the Becel Heart Health Information Bureau has been helping Canadians learn about heart health. Becel believes that with sufficient information and a little encouragement you can improve the health of your heart. Becel's *HeartHealthy Cooking* has been designed to complement your efforts to lead a heart healthy lifestyle.

Throughout the pages of this cookbook you will find:
- information about following a diet that is good for your heart, including choosing unsaturated fats more often and limiting your intake of saturated fat and trans fat.
- delicious recipes for everyday dining and special occasions.
- grocery shopping, label reading, cooking and food preparation tips and ideas.
- tips on how to make permanent food and lifestyle behaviour changes.

The Becel Heart Health Information Bureau would like to thank the following individuals who contributed both time and talent:
Recipe Development: Susan Bailey, Food Consultant, P.H.Ec.
Yvonne Tremblay, Food Consultant/Nutritionist, Joan Ttooulias, Home Economics Consultant, P.H.Ec.; Heather Trim, Food Consultant.
Dietitian writers: Wendy Benson, RD MPH; Chantal Blais, PDt.; Leah Hawriko, RDN; Liz Pearson, RD.
There are always individuals who work behind the scenes and deserve thanks and credit for the final result; Ross Hugessen, Jan Mollenhauer, David Jacobs, Kevin Ryan, Ruth Millar, Andrea Bock and Peter Maher (from Key Porter Books), Pete Paterson, Sue Henderson and Catherine MacFayden. We would like to thank Drs. Nancy Schwartz and Elaine Letendre for their contributions and review. Special thanks to Sharon Joliat, M.Sc., RD, President, Info Access (1988) Inc. for providing nutrient analysis for the recipes and always being available to answer questions.

If you would like more information about heart health and nutrition we invite you visit the Becel web site at **www.becelcanada.com** for information about the importance of nutrition to help reduce your risk for heart disease and food preparation tips and recipes. Look for Your Personal Food Diary™, a diary to monitor your current diet as it relates to *Canada's Food Guide to Healthy Eating* and a more heart healthy way of eating.

Becel Heart Health Information Bureau
Barbara Ledermann, MSc., RD
Bridget Wilson , P.H.Ec.

Contents

Foreword

Many Canadians often feel overwhelmed and confused by all of the seemingly contradictory news reports that link food and nutrition to health and disease. If the latest headlines leave you hungry for some good news about food and health, consider these facts:

1. Enjoying delicious food is, and should be, one of life's greatest pleasures.
2. Healthy eating can be tasty and enjoyable in addition to being good for you.
3. Healthy eating is an important key to a healthy heart.

Now Becel®* brings you *HeartHealthy Cooking: Delicious Everyday Recipes*—a cookbook that is firmly based on these three facts. Combining authoritative and practical nutrition information with easy, creative heart healthy recipes, Becel's *HeartHealthy Cooking* is written for people who want to achieve and maintain a more hearthealthy eating style without sacrificing taste or spending too much time in the kitchen. In short, Becel's *HeartHealthy Cooking* is full of good news both for your heart and for your taste buds.

For most people, hearthealthy eating is a two-step process. First, we limit the total amount of fat, especially saturated fat, that we eat. Then we focus on the *kinds* of fat we eat (i.e., emphasizing healthier fats over less healthy fats). A hearthealthy diet doesn't mean depriving yourself of the nutrients, taste and smooth texture that fats add to food, it only means making the right food choices.

Contrary to popular belief, fat is an essential nutrient, and unnecessarily limiting fat intake can actually be harmful to your health. However, all fats are not created equal. Healthy eating involves making wise food choices to ensure a healthy balance in both the amount and the kinds of fat we eat.

But hearthealthy eating is not achieved by attention to fat alone. The nutrition tips and recipes in this book reflect the sound principles of *Canada's Food Guide to Healthy Eating* and thus promote a varied and balanced eating style to support overall health and well-being.

* ®Becel is a registered trademark of Lipton, Toronto, ON. Canada M4W 3R2

Following the advice and recipes in Becel's *HeartHealthy Eating* will help you to achieve the following goals:

- be realistic by making small, manageable changes in your eating style over time;
- be adventurous by expanding your tastes to include a broader variety of foods;
- be sensible by enjoying all foods in reasonable amounts without over-doing it;
- be flexible by balancing your food choices and physical activity over several days.

Healthy eating, along with regular physical activity, can be one of the best personal investments you can make towards enhancing your health and well-being. I encourage you to make the most of the opportunity that the combination of healthy eating and regular exercise offers and I hope that this book will provide the necessary fuel for this delicious journey.

Nancy E. Schwartz, PhD, FDC
Nutrition Consultant
Oakville, Ontario

About the Nutrient Values in this Book

Nutrient Analysis was performed by Info Access (1988) Inc., Don Mills, Ontario, using the nutritional accouting component of the CBORD Menu Management System. The nutrient database was the 1997 Canadian Nutrient File, supplemented when necessary with documented data from reliable sources.

Analysis was based on:

- imperial weights and measures (except for foods typically packaged and used in metric quantity);
- the smaller number of servings (i.e. larger portions) when there was a range;
- the first ingredient when there was a choice.

Calculations of meat and poultry recipes assumed that only the lean flesh portion was eaten. Optional ingredients and ingredients in unspecified amounts were not included in the analysis.

Nutrient information on recipes: nutrient values were rounded to one decimal place. Good and excellent sources of vitamins and minerals, and description of dietary fibre content, have been included and were based on the criteria established for nutition labelling (Guide to Food Labelling and Advertising, Agriculture and Agri-Food Canada, March 1996).

When baking or cooking with margarine, be sure to follow the recipe instructions. Since Becel light margarine contains half the fat (and therefore more moisture) of regular Becel margarine, it will perform differently in recipes and cooking applications. Replacing regular Becel with Becel light (or vice versa) will affect the quality of your baked goods. To ensure the best result, use the type of margarine called for in the recipe.

Legend:
Understanding the Nutrition Information
SFA = saturated fat
PUFA = polyunsaturated fat
MUFA = monounsaturated fat

The Basics of HeartHealthy Eating

Your Incredible Heart

Your heart—your body's hardest-working muscle—is a truly magnificent machine. It pumps blood through an amazing 113,000-kilometre network of blood vessels. It allows your blood to deliver life-sustaining oxygen and essential nutrients to your cells and to carry away waste products like carbon dioxide. It beats an average of 100,000 times each day.

Heart disease, a broad term that describes diseases of the heart and blood vessels, is a problem of enormous magnitude.

- Heart disease is the leading cause of death in Canada.
- More than one-third of Canadians die of heart disease.
- Women are just as vulnerable to heart disease as men, although it tends to appear 6 to 10 years later in women.
- Heart disease is not limited to the elderly—it is a major cause of death for people under the age of 75.
- Heart disease can have a major impact on a person's quality of life, bringing chronic pain or discomfort, restricting activities and causing disability and unemployment.*

What's Your Risk?

Although age and family history influence your risk of heart disease, the way you live also affects your risk. Unhealthy habits over time cause atherosclerosis—the build-up of fatty deposits or plaque on the artery walls. Clogged or narrowed arteries can lead to a heart attack or stroke.

Extensive research has shown that watching the following modifiable factors can reduce your risk of heart disease:

* *The Changing Face of Heart Disease and Stroke in Canada 2000*, Heart and Stroke Foundation of Canada, October 1999.

Smoking. Smoking causes injury to artery walls and increases the rate at which plaque builds up.

High blood cholesterol. As blood cholesterol levels increase, more plaque builds up on artery walls.

High blood pressure. High blood pressure increases the heart's workload, causing the heart to enlarge and weaken over time.

Obesity and excess weight. Excess body weight increases the strain on your heart. It also increases your risk of high blood pressure, high blood cholesterol and Type 2 diabetes.

Physical inactivity. Lack of physical activity affects heart health in many ways. For example, if you are inactive you are more likely to suffer from high blood cholesterol, high blood pressure, obesity and Type 2 diabetes—and all of these, in turn, increase your risk of heart disease.

Healthy Eating for a Healthy Heart

What you eat significantly influences your risk of high blood cholesterol, high blood pressure and obesity. In other words, a healthy diet is critical for a healthy heart. Narrowing of the arteries can be slowed down—and even reversed in some cases—by choosing healthy foods and making other lifestyle changes.

Here are the three basics of heart healthy eating:

1. Watch the amount and type of fat.

Enjoy a lower-fat diet but also be sure to choose fats that are healthier for your heart; quality is as important as quantity. According to nutrition experts, no more than 30 percent of your total calories each day should come from fat. Reduce your intake of saturated and trans fats (which tend to increase blood cholesterol) and replace them with monounsaturated and polyunsaturated fats (which help lower blood cholesterol).

The following information will help you make healthier choices:

Type of fat	Heart healthy?	Source
Saturated fats	X	Foods that mostly come from animal sources—including higher-fat meats and milk products such as cheese and butter.
Trans fats	X	Many processed foods containing partially hydrogenated fats, such as cookies and crackers, as well as deep-fried foods and hard margarines. These fats also naturally occur in milk, butter and meat.
Monounsaturated fats	✓	Olive and canola oils, foods such as soft margarines (containing these oils), nuts, seeds, avocados and olives.
Polyunsaturated fats	✓	Sunflower, corn, safflower and soybean oils. Foods such as soft margarines (containing these oils), nuts and seeds.
Omega-3 fats	✓	Particularly healthy for your heart. Found in canola oil, walnuts, flaxseed, some soft margarines (made from canola oil) and higher-fat fish such as salmon and trout.

Dietary cholesterol is found in foods such as eggs, high-fat milk products, processed and organ meats and shellfish. For some people, eating foods rich in dietary cholesterol causes their blood cholesterol levels to rise. For most people, however, the emphasis should be on lowering saturated and trans fat while consuming dietary cholesterol in moderation.

2. Choose high-fibre foods more often.

Aim to consume 25 to 30 grams of fibre each day by making whole grains, beans, vegetables and fruit a regular part of your diet. These foods contain antioxidants and various plant compounds that further reduce your risk of heart disease. Both soluble and insoluble fibre are important for good health.

- soluble fibre helps lower the risk of heart disease by lowering blood cholesterol levels. It is found in oats, beans, barley and pectin-rich fruits such as apples and citrus fruits;
- insoluble fibre helps regulate bowel movements and prevent constipation. It is found in whole wheat breads and cereals, vegetables and fruit.

3. Use salt sparingly.

For some people, too much salt can cause high blood pressure. To reduce your salt intake:

- minimize or eliminate the use of salt in food preparation—do not add salt to food at the table;
- decrease your use of canned goods, snack foods, frozen dinners, pickles, crackers, cheese, cold cuts and fast foods;
- buy salt-reduced versions of your favourite products whenever possible;
- be creative and experiment with different herbs, spices and other flavour enhancers, like onions and garlic;
- use sour flavours to replace salty flavours—for example, squeeze lemon juice on salads, cooked vegetables, fish and pasta.

Getting enough vegetables, fruit and low-fat milk products will also help moderate your blood pressure.

The Specifics of HeartHealthy Eating

A heart healthy diet is based on *Canada's Food Guide to Healthy Eating*. It means enjoying a diet rich in whole grains, beans, vegetables and fruit in combination with modest portions of lean meats and lower-fat milk

Health Canada   **Santé Canada**

CANADA'S Food Guide
TO HEALTHY EATING
FOR PEOPLE FOUR YEARS AND OVER

Enjoy a variety
of foods from each
group every day.

Choose lower-
fat foods
more often.

Grain Products
Choose whole grain
and enriched prod-
ucts more often.

Vegetables and Fruit
Choose dark green and
orange vegetables and
orange fruit more often.

Milk Products
Choose lower-fat milk
products more often.

Meat and Alternatives
Choose leaner meats,
poultry and fish, as well
as dried peas, beans
and lentils more often.

Canada

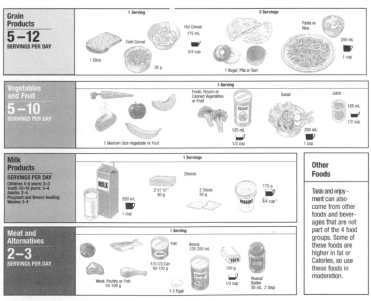

Grain Products
5–12 SERVINGS PER DAY

1 Serving — 1 Slice — Cold Cereal 30 g — Hot Cereal 175 mL 3/4 cup
2 Servings — 1 Bagel, Pita or Bun — Pasta or Rice 250 mL 1 cup

Vegetables and Fruit
5–10 SERVINGS PER DAY

1 Serving — 1 Medium Size Vegetable or Fruit — Fresh, Frozen or Canned Vegetables or Fruit 125 mL 1/2 cup — Salad 250 mL 1 cup — Juice 125 mL 1/2 cup

Milk Products
SERVINGS PER DAY
Children 4–9 years: 2–3
Youth 10–16 years: 3–4
Adults: 2–4
Pregnant and Breast-feeding Women 3–4

1 Servings — Milk 250 mL 1 cup — Cheese 3"x1"x1" 50 g — 2 Slices 50 g — Yogurt 175 g 3/4 cup

Other Foods

Taste and enjoy-
ment can also
come from other
foods and bever-
ages that are not
part of the 4 food
groups. Some of
these foods are
higher in fat or
Calories, so use
these foods in
moderation.

Meat and Alternatives
2–3 SERVINGS PER DAY

1 Serving — Meat, Poultry or Fish 50–100 g — Fish 1/3–2/3 Can 50–100 g — 1–2 Eggs — Beans 125–250 mL — Tofu 100 g 1/3 cup — Peanut Butter 30 mL 2 tbsp

Different People Need Different Amounts of Food
The amount of food you need every day from the 4 food groups and other foods depends on your age, body size, activity
level, whether you are male or female and if you are pregnant or breast-feeding. That's why the Food Guide gives a lower and
higher number of servings for each food group. For example, young children can choose the lower number of servings, while
male teenagers can go to the higher number. Most other people can choose servings somewhere in between.

products; this ensures that you get all the essential nutrients required for good health.

Canada's Food Guide to Healthy Eating provides a maximum and minimum number of recommended servings for each food group. The amount of food you need each day depends on your age, body size, activity level and whether you are male or female (either pregnant or not). Young children can choose the lower number of servings, while active male teenagers can choose the higher number. Most other people can choose servings somewhere in between. Here's a closer look at each food group.

Grain Products

Breads, cereals, pasta, rice.
Enjoy 5 to 12 servings each day.

Heart healthy examples of a single serving include:

- 1 slice of whole grain bread or ½ bagel or bun.
- ½ cup (125 mL) cooked whole wheat pasta or brown rice.
- ½ cup (125 mL) cooked oatmeal.

Serving-size Tip: A large plate of pasta counts as 3 or 4 servings. A small bagel or hamburger bun counts as 2 servings.

Healthy Eating Tips

- choose 100% whole wheat or whole grain breads.
- buy whole grain cereals with 3 to 4 grams of fibre per serving.
- sprinkle hot or cold cereal with oat or wheat bran for extra fibre.
- enjoy whole wheat pasta, brown rice and wild rice more often.
- try whole grain couscous, bulgur, barley, millet and quinoa instead of rice for a change.
- cook pasta, rice and hot cereals without adding salt to the water. Limit your intake of instant and ready-to-eat varieties of these foods, which contain higher amounts of salt.

Vegetables and Fruit

Fresh, frozen, canned or as juice.
Enjoy 5 to 10 servings each day.

Heart healthy examples of a single serving include:

- 1 medium-size or ½ cup (125 mL) raw or cooked vegetables or fruit.
- 1 cup (250 mL) dark green leafy salad.

Serving-size Tip: A single serving of vegetables or fruit is about the size of a tennis ball.

Healthy Eating Tips

- for maximum nutrition, choose dark green, red and orange vegetables and fruit more often (such as spinach, broccoli, oranges, carrots, red peppers and strawberries).
- choose whole vegetables and fruit rather than fruit and vegetable juices, which contain very little fibre. Fruit juice is also high in calories and many tomato juices are high in salt.
- choose fresh or frozen vegetables more often. Most canned vegetables are high in salt.
- choose from all the vegetables and fruit available. The only exception is coconut, which is high in saturated fat.
- olives and avocados are high in fat, though the fat is mostly unsaturated. Watch your serving sizes to control calories, particularly if you are trying to reduce or control your weight.

Milk Products

Milk, yogurt, cheese.
Enjoy 2 to 4 servings each day.

Heart healthy examples of a single serving include:

- 1 cup (250 mL) skim or 1% milk.
- 50 grams or 2 slices of lower-fat cheese.
- ¾ cup (175 g) 1% or low-fat yogurt.

Serving-size Tip: A 50-gram piece of cheese is about the size of an adult's thumb.

Healthy Eating Tips

- choose lower-fat milk, cheese and yogurt more often.
- choose lower-fat frozen yogurt and ice cream.

Meat and Alternatives
Meat, fish, beans, tofu, nuts, peanut butter.
Enjoy 2 to 3 servings each day.

Heart healthy examples of a single serving include:

- 1 $^3/_4$ oz to 3 $^1/_2$ oz (50 to 100 grams) lean meat, poultry, fish or tofu.
- $^1/_2$ cup to 1 cup (125 to 250 mL) cooked beans.
- 2 tablespoons (30 mL) nuts, seeds or peanut butter.
- 1 to 2 eggs (maximum 3 to 4 yolks per week).

Serving-size Tip: A 3-oz (100-gram) serving of meat, fish or poultry is about the size of a deck of cards.

Healthy Eating Tips

- choose lean meats such as chicken breasts and drumsticks without the skin, pork tenderloin, and "round" or "loin" cuts of beef more often. Trim meat of all visible fat.
- when using ground meat, brown and drain off all the fat before adding to foods like chili, spaghetti sauce or shepherd's pie.
- limit your use of high-fat processed meat products such as bologna, salami, hot dogs, sausages and bacon by choosing the low-fat or lean versions of these meat products or choose chicken, turkey or fish whenever possible.
- at least twice a week, enjoy fish that is high in Omega-3 fats, such as trout or salmon. Limit your intake of breaded or battered fish that is deep-fried.

- moderate your intake of shellfish (such as shrimp). Although low in saturated fat, shellfish is higher in cholesterol than other types of seafood.
- choose dried peas, beans and lentils regularly. When using canned beans, reduce the salt by draining the liquid and rinsing the beans with water.
- nuts (such as almonds, walnuts and peanuts) and seeds (such as sesame and sunflower) can be part of a heart healthy diet if consumed in small quantities. A small handful is equal to one serving. Choose unsalted varieties instead of salted.

Other Foods

Oils, margarines, jams, syrups, sugar, spices, condiments, coffee, tea and other beverages, snack foods, candy, cakes, cookies and other desserts.

These foods, although they do not belong to one of the 4 food groups, are important because they help provide taste and enjoyment to foods. They should be used in moderation, especially if you need to reduce your body weight.

Healthy Eating Tips

- many of these foods can be used to enhance the taste and enjoyment of food. For example, enjoy a small amount of soft, non-hydrogenated margarine on cooked vegetables, or jam on whole wheat toast.
- stir-fry rather than deep-fry your foods. Broil, bake, roast, poach, microwave and steam foods regularly.
- choose a margarine that is soft, non-hydrogenated and low in saturated fat. Reduced-fat and reduced-salt varieties are also available.
- enjoy low-fat condiments such as mustard and ketchup. Use low-fat mayonnaise and salad dressing instead of the full-fat varieties.
- be sensible. Enjoy small amounts of your favourite desserts and snacks on occasion. Choose low-fat desserts and salt-reduced snack foods whenever possible.
- be flexible. Choosing a higher-fat food or meal from time to time will not make or break your health. Just remember to balance higher-fat choices with lower-fat ones. For example, if your day includes one higher-fat meal, make sure your other meals are low in fat (or eat two

lighter meals that day). Alternatively, balance the fats in a meal by combining one higher-fat food with other lower-fat foods. Exercise can also balance the occasional indulgence—simply be more active that day.

An Important Reminder

To keep your heart healthy, it's important to stay active and maintain a healthy weight. Aim for at least 30 minutes of a moderately intense activity (like brisk walking) on most days of the week. If you need to lose weight, don't be overwhelmed. For many people, losing as little as 10 to 20 pounds (5 to 9 kilograms) can make a big difference.

Here's to a happy, healthy heart!

Liz Pearson, RD
Toronto

A Closer Look at the Foods We Eat

Food as Energy

Your body is a complex machine that requires energy to function. Energy enables your body to carry out basic functions such as absorbing and digesting food and making your muscles work as well as giving it the ability to respond to environmental stresses. Your body absorbs energy (which is measured in calories) from the nutrients in the food you eat. That is why understanding the role nutrients play in your diet is an important step in making healthy eating choices.

The Nutrient Spectrum

Fat, carbohydrates and protein—the "macronutrients"—are essential food nutrients. The body uses fat and carbohydrates primarily for energy, and protein is essential for forming and repairing the body's tissues. Other nutrients, such as vitamins and minerals—the "micronutrients"— are present in smaller quantities. Micronutrients are needed in small amounts to promote growth and maintain life.

The Facts on Dietary Fats

Fats are an essential part of your diet. Not only do they add flavour to food but they also provide important nutrients. Fats insulate and protect the body's vital organs. Without fat, your body would not be able to receive or use important vitamins such as A, D, E and K. Fats are also a source of essential fats, which are not produced by our bodies but necessary for a healthy heart and for cell building and hormone production.

How much fat should you eat?

Nutrition experts' current recommendations suggest that 30 percent or less of our total calories should come from fat. As a general rule, the average woman should eat no more than 65 grams of fat per day, and the average man should eat no more than 90 grams.

Of the fat we eat, it is recommended that monounsaturated and polyunsaturated fats should make up the larger portion, and that saturated and trans fats should be reduced as much as possible, to no more than 10 percent of daily calories.

Fats are not all alike. There are different types of fat: saturated, unsaturated (polyunsaturated and monounsaturated) and trans fat. These different types of fat have different effects on your body and on your health.

Saturated fat

Saturated fat has been shown to increase the level of low density lipoprotein (LDL), or "bad" cholesterol, in the blood. This type of fat is mostly found in animal products such as meat, poultry skin and milk products. Fats that are solid at room temperature (such as butter, shortening, hard margarine, palm or coconut oil and partially hydrogenated oils) contain saturated fat.

Unsaturated fat

Unsaturated fats actively lower blood cholesterol. They are found in vegetable oils and are soft at room temperature. They are the healthy fats that provide the essential fats important for good health. Try to choose sources of unsaturated fat whenever possible. Unsaturated fats are divided into 2 categories (both have been shown to reduce LDL cholesterol in the blood):

- **monounsaturated fats**, which are found mostly in vegetable oils and products made with these oils (such as olive and canola oils);
- **polyunsaturated fats**, which are liquid at room temperature and are mostly found in vegetable oils made from corn, sunflower, soybean and safflower oils, as well as in soft, non-hydrogenated margarine made from these oils.

Polyunsaturated fats are also a source of essential fats—specifically Omega-6 and Omega-3—that come from vegetable oils and fish.

Omega-3 fat has been shown to reduce triglycerides, a type of fat found in the blood. High levels of triglycerides often appear with other well-known heart disease risk factors, such as high blood cholesterol and diabetes. Omega-3 fat (found in fatty fish such as salmon, trout, mackerel and sardines; walnuts and canola, flaxseed and soybean oils and foods made from these oils) offers many other benefits, including reducing the risk of blood clots, which helps to reduce the risk of heart disease and stroke.

Trans fat

Trans fat—also known as trans fatty acids—is found in many foods that contain shortening or partially hydrogenated fats (such as cookies, crackers, french fries and some margarines). Trans fat also occurs naturally in milk, butter and meat. (Hydrogenation is a way to harden liquid vegetable oils and make them firmer. Vegetable oils that have been hydrogenated tend to have more saturated fat and, in the case of partial hydrogenation, more trans fat.)

Both saturated fat and trans fat have been shown to increase blood cholesterol and consumption should be limited as much as possible.

Cholesterol

Cholesterol is a waxy substance produced by the liver. It is normally found in the blood and in body tissue. Although cholesterol is essential for a healthy body, excess amounts in the blood can lead to hardening of the arteries and heart disease.

There are two types of cholesterol. Blood cholesterol is the level of cholesterol measured in the blood. Dietary cholesterol is the cholesterol that occurs naturally in food.

Generally speaking, 80 percent of the cholesterol found in our bodies is produced by the liver. The remaining 20 percent is obtained from food. The principal sources of dietary cholesterol include egg yolks and organ meats, but cholesterol is also found in poultry, fish and both the lean and fatty parts of meat. In milk products, cholesterol and saturated fat are proportional to the level of fat. For example, low-fat milk, such as skim or 1%, contains little saturated fat and little or no cholesterol.

For some people, eating foods rich in dietary cholesterol can lead to an increase in blood cholesterol. But for most people, it is important to reduce the consumption of trans fat and saturated fat and to limit foods containing cholesterol.

Carbohydrates for Energy

Carbohydrates are the body's main source of energy. This is because carbohydrates are easily and quickly digested and produce energy that is readily available to fuel our bodies. That is why it is no surprise our diet is made up primarily of carbohydrates. Carbohydrates represent anywhere from 50 to 70 percent of our total calories consumed.

Fibre

For a healthy diet, Health Canada recommends that carbohydrates—particularly complex carbohydrates—account for up to 55 percent of our total daily calories. They're readily available in many food groups, but first choice should be given to fruit and vegetables, whole grain breads and

Maintaining a Healthy Weight

The amount of energy you need depends on your body size, gender, age and activity level. When the amount of food you eat corresponds to your body's needs, a balance of energy is achieved. This results in a stable body weight. If you eat more food than your body can use, your weight goes up; if you don't eat enough, your weight falls.

How much should you weigh? The Body Mass Index (BMI) is a tool used by health professionals to assess a healthy body weight. The BMI is a formula based on your height and weight. For optimal health, try to maintain a Body Mass Index between 20 and 25. To find out your BMI, take your weight (in kilograms) and divide it by your height (in metres) squared:

$$\frac{\text{Weight (kg)}}{\text{Height (m)}^2} = \text{BMI} \qquad \frac{70}{1.7 \times 1.7} = 24.22$$

cereals and legumes. These carbohydrates have the additional benefit of being rich in dietary fibre. Foods that are rich in fibre are recommended for controlling constipation, blood sugar (for people with diabetes) and appetite. Fibre also helps to reduce blood cholesterol. If you're trying to increase the fibre in your diet, it's best to make changes slowly. Sudden increases may cause bloating, cramps or diarrhea. Always remember to drink plenty of water.

Other Carbohydrates

Sweets, such as sugar and honey, contain a significant number of calories but relatively few other nutrients. This is because they contain primarily simple carbohydrates. Sweets do add taste and enjoyment to eating, but should be consumed in smaller amounts, especially if you are trying to reduce or control your weight.

For example, a person who is 1.7 metres tall and weighs 70 kilograms would have a BMI of 24, which falls into the healthy range:

$$\frac{70}{1.7 \times 1.7} = 24.22$$

Distribution of body fat is another consideration. The accumulation of abdominal fat is a recognized risk factor for heart disease. Measuring your waist-hip ratio (WHR) is a useful indicator of your body fat distribution. Apple-shaped people (excess fat around the abdomen) generally have a greater risk of heart disease than pear-shaped people (excess fat around the hips).

To determine your waist-hip ratio, divide your waist circumference (in centimetres) by your hip circumference (in centimetres):

$$WHR = \frac{waist\ (cm)}{hips\ (cm)}$$

Women should aim for a waist-hip ratio less than 0.8, and men for less than 0.9.

Proteins, the Building Blocks of Growth

Your body requires protein for the growth and maintenance of body tissue. Each gram of protein contains just 4 calories of energy. However, the energy provided by protein is not used as easily as the energy from carbohydrates and fats.

How to get the protein, with less fat

Meat, chicken and fish all contain protein and are often considered the foundation of the meal. However, the protein provided by meat and milk products is always accompanied by saturated fat. To get the protein you need and still monitor your total fat intake, choose skim milk products, trimmed lean meat and fish and skinless poultry, and generally limit the serving size of meat.

Even though eating foods that contain protein at every meal is recommended, it is not necessary to have meat more than once a day, or even every day. Nuts, legumes, eggs, tofu and its derivatives are just some of the protein-rich meat alternatives available. They are also an excellent source of dietary fibre.

Chantal Blais, PDt
Montreal

Grocery Shopping and Label Reading

HeartHealthy Grocery Shopping

Can busy people eat well? Yes! The key to success is to keep your cupboard shelves and refrigerator well stocked with healthy staples. Staple foods will enable you to balance the occasional dietary indulgence. It's fine to indulge in moderation, but for heart-healthier eating it's important to pay attention to both the amount and type of fat in food. Keep the four food groups in mind when you go grocery shopping (see page 13). Learning how to read the nutrition labels on packages also makes it easier to choose healthier products.

To find out just how "hearthealthy" your shopping is right now, take the quiz on the following page. Then take a close look at the questions to which you answered "Never," "Seldom" and "Sometimes" to discover where you can make improvements. These are areas where you can make changes for the better.

If you answered "Often" or "Always" to any question, congratulations! You already have some hearthealthy shopping routines.

Is there room for improvement? With a little planning and the right information, it's easy to make small daily changes that will make your diet healthier:

- **Plan ahead.** Being organized saves you time and minimizes extra trips to the store. Plan to add one or two new heart healthy meals each week to your repertoire.
- **Make a list.** Impulse purchases are often not the best food choices. To avoid impulse buying, stick to your list as much as possible and never shop on an empty stomach.
- **Set realistic goals.** Try to increase fibre, for example. A simple way to boost fibre in your diet is to choose a breakfast cereal that has 4 grams of fibre per serving. You could also try cooking with brown rice instead of white.

How heart healthy is your shopping right now?
Take this quiz and find out.

1) Do fruit and vegetables account for at least 25 percent of the food items on your shopping list?

   ☐ never   ☐ seldom   ☐ sometimes   ☐ often   ☐ always

2) On average, do grain products (breads, pasta, rice, cereals) make up at least 25 percent of the food items on your shopping list?

   ☐ never   ☐ seldom   ☐ sometimes   ☐ often   ☐ always

3) When you buy milk products, do you choose lower-fat varieties?

   ☐ never   ☐ seldom   ☐ sometimes   ☐ often   ☐ always

4) When you buy meat, do you select lean cuts and smaller portions?

   ☐ never   ☐ seldom   ☐ sometimes   ☐ often   ☐ always

5) How often do you purchase legumes, beans or tofu?

   ☐ never   ☐ seldom   ☐ sometimes   ☐ often   ☐ always

6) When you buy margarine, do you choose one that is soft, non-hydrogenated and low in saturated fat?

   ☐ never   ☐ seldom   ☐ sometimes   ☐ often   ☐ always

7) When comparing similar foods, do you read the labels?

   ☐ never   ☐ seldom   ☐ sometimes   ☐ often   ☐ always

(Adapted from "Shopping for Heart Health," a publication of the Becel Heart Health Information Bureau. For more heart health shopping tips and advice, visit www.becelcanada.com).

Grocery Shopping and Label Reading

Navigating the Supermarket

Once you have your list in hand, you're ready to shop. These 5 guidelines will help you stick to the basics and not be overwhelmed by all the choices.

1. Purchase mostly fresh fruit and vegetables instead of canned produce.
2. Choose foods made from whole wheat and whole grains instead of refined white flour. For example, choose whole grain breakfast cereals and whole wheat bread rather than sugar-based cereals and white bread.
3. It is not only the total fat you eat that matters, but the kinds of fat. Choose foods where most of the fat is unsaturated.
4. Compare product labels for serving size, fat content (both quality and quantity of fat), fibre, sugar and salt.
5. Aim for variety among the 4 food groups in *Canada's Food Guide to Healthy Eating* (page 13).

How to Read Nutrition Labels

Reading the nutrition information label is the best way to understand what's in a product. Here's a look at what you'll find on the label.

NUTRITION INFORMATION NUTRITIONNELLE PER 10g (2 tsp) SERVING / PAR PORTION DE 10 g (2 c à thé)		% OF RECOMMENDED DAILY INTAKE/ % DE L'APPORT QUOTIDIEN RECOMMANDÉ	
Energy / Énergie	73 Cal/310 kJ	AN EXCELLENT SOURCE OF VITAMIN D. A GOOD SOURCE OF VITAMIN E. UNE EXCELLENTE SOURCE DE VITAMINE D. UNE BONNE SOURCE DE VITAMINE E.	
Protein / Protéines	0 g		
Fat / Matières grasses	8.0 g	Vitamin A / Vitamine A	11%
⌈ Polyunsaturates / Polyinsaturés	3.3 g	Vitamin D / Vitamine D	28%
⌊ Monounsaturates / Monoinsaturés	3.3 g	Vitamin E / Vitamine E	18%
Saturates / Saturés	1.1 g		
Trans Fat / Gras trans	0.1 g ✦	✦ **Virtually No Trans Fat**	
Cholesterol / Cholestérol	0 mg	**Pratiquement pas de gras trans**	
Carbohydrate / Glucides	0 1 g		

Nutrition information panel

The nutrition information panel lists the food energy (calories), fat content (quantity and quality) and amount of fibre provided by a single serving. It is the most precise way to determine the nutritional value of a food. When comparing labels, always check the serving size, to make sure you're comparing similar portions.

Other items that frequently appear on food products would be:

Ingredient list

The ingredient list on packaged foods presents the ingredients in descending order by weight. Words ending in "ose" (e.g., sucrose) are sugars. "Sodium" is salt. Consulting the ingredient list is essential if you have food allergies.

Nutrient content claims

Nutrition claims are statements that summarize a product's key nutritional features. But they don't always tell the whole story. For example, a product claiming to be a "very high source of fibre" may also be high in saturated fat or sugar. Consult the nutrition information panel to be sure of what's inside.

Leah Hawirko, RDN
North Vancouver

What's for Dinner?

Meal Planning

Now that all those great, healthy foods are home from the grocery store, what's the best way to serve them?

Start planning your menu with *Canada's Food Guide to Healthy Eating* in mind (see page 13). Picture your meal on the table. Three-quarters of the foods should be grains, vegetables and fruit. Add colour to your meal—especially with orange, red or dark green vegetables or fruits. Add meat or protein alternatives (such as legumes or tofu) to complement the grains and vegetables. Include milk products, such as skim or 1% milk, and a heart healthy dessert such as lower-fat milk pudding.

Fat can be part of a healthy diet and add flavour to your meal. Using soft, non-hydrogenated margarine and vegetable oil is an easy way to help increase polyunsaturated, monounsaturated and essential fats in your diet. Use them for frying or sautéing, and use vegetable oils in salad dressings.

So Much Information! Where Do I Start?

The conflicting nutritional advice you get from magazines, newspapers and television can be overwhelming once you decide to change your diet. Nevertheless, health experts agree that if you change your food choices slowly and steadily, you are more likely to make healthy changes a permanent part of your lifestyle.

Think back over the last 2 to 3 years. What healthy eating changes have you made? Perhaps you switched to skim or 1% milk, or started using a non-hydrogenated margarine. Think about how you made that change. Was it fairly straightforward? Did you experiment before finding the right foods for you? Most people go through a trial-and-error phase before a diet change becomes a permanent habit.

As you move towards a lower-fat, higher-fibre diet, remember that there are no bad foods. It's okay to enjoy a higher-fat meal once in a while. It's the combination of meals and snacks you eat during the day or week that is more important than any one food or meal.

Steps to Healthy Eating: Your Checklist

The checklist below is a useful summary of heart healthy eating habits. Read through it, and check which of the habits you already follow and which ones you need to practise more often.

Heart Healthy Checklist

Some of these suggestions may not apply to people who have food allergies or other health concerns, or to people who choose a vegetarian or vegan diet. Choose the suggestions that work for you.

I Do This Often		I Could Do This More Often
Grain products		
_____	• Use grains to make up about $\frac{1}{4}$ to $\frac{1}{2}$ of every meal.	_____
_____	• Eat brown rice or whole wheat pasta and eat whole wheat bread regularly.	_____
_____	• Include higher-fibre cereals (more than 4 grams of fibre per serving) in my regular diet.	_____
_____	• Eat doughnuts, pastries or muffins only occasionally.	_____
Vegetables and fruit		
_____	• Ensure vegetables and fruit make up at least $\frac{1}{4}$ of every meal.	_____
_____	• Eat dark green, orange and red vegetables and fruits regularly.	_____
_____	• Serve fruit-based desserts such as fruit salad, apple crisp or baked or poached pears.	_____

Milk products

_____   • Choose skim or 1% milk and yogurt.   _____

_____   • Choose lower-fat cheeses
(less than 20% MF), such as partly
skimmed mozzarella.   _____

Meat and alternatives

_____   • Keep lean meats, poultry and fish lower-fat
by roasting, barbecuing, poaching, broiling
or frying with a little oil or soft,
non-hydrogenated margarine.   _____

_____   • From the deli counter, choose leaner meats
such as ham, roast beef, chicken or turkey.   _____

_____   • Choose modest-sized servings of meat
(about the size of a deck of cards).   _____

Other foods

_____   • Use soft, non-hydrogenated margarine
or vegetable oils in moderation at the
table and in cooking.   _____

_____   • Eat lower-fat snacks such as popcorn or
bagel chips instead of potato chips or
nachos.   _____

_____   • Eat sherbets or low-fat ice cream
occasionally.   _____

Making changes, one step at a time

First, give yourself a pat on the back for all the heart healthy food habits you already have! Now consider the items that you selected as "I Could Do This More Often." Choose 2 or 3 habits from this list that you can change right now to make your diet lower in fat and higher in fibre. Every 6 weeks or so, review this list again and work in 2 or 3 other foods. In 2 to 4 months, you will be on your way to a heart healthy diet.

Once you have decided what to work on, develop a concrete plan that's practical for *you*. Use the recipes in this book for inspiration and to help you build the healthy eating habits you want. Remember that modifying your diet can take time, especially when you want the change to become permanent.

Healthy eating can be fun, easy and delicious. Remember, you are working towards having more energy, better weight control, improved blood cholesterol levels—and a healthier heart!

Wendy Benson, RD, MPH
Calgary

Appetizers and Snacks

Fast

When You Have More Time

Roasted Red Pepper Crostini

These colourful appetizers will be a hit at your next party. Garlic-rubbed baguette slices may be prepared a week in advance and stored in an airtight container at room temperature. Peppers may be roasted a couple of days in advance, tossed with vinegar and herbs, then covered and refrigerated. Assemble the crostini just before serving or they will become soggy.

Preparation: 15 minutes
Cooking Time: 25 minutes
Makes 30 appetizers

2	large sweet red peppers	2
2 tbsp	finely chopped basil or parsley	30 mL
1 tsp	balsamic vinegar (optional)	5 mL
	Salt and freshly ground black pepper to taste	
1	thin baguette, about 10 inches (25 cm)	1
2 tsp	Becel margarine, melted	10 mL
1	large clove garlic, cut in half	1
1/4 cup	creamy goat cheese	50 mL

Nutrients per serving
(1 piece)
Calories 40
Protein 1.4 g
Fat 1 g
  PUFA 0.2 g
  MUFA 0.3 g
  SFA 0.4 g
Carbohydrates 6.3 g
Fibre 0.3 g
Cholesterol 1 mg
Sodium 68 mg
Potassium 28 mg
Good source of vitamin C.

Preheat broiler. Place peppers on a baking sheet, about 4 inches (10 cm) from broiler. Broil until blackened on all sides, turning occasionally, 8 to 10 minutes. Remove from oven; cover with a clean tea towel until shrivelled and cool enough to handle, about 10 minutes. Peel peppers with a small knife, remove seeds and cut into julienne strips 1 inch (4 cm) long. Toss peppers with basil, balsamic vinegar (if using), salt and pepper.

Preheat oven to 400°F (200°C). Cut baguette into 1/4-inch (5-mm) slices. Slices should be bite-sized (about 1 1/2 inches/4 cm); cut slices in half if necessary. You will need 30 slices. Lightly brush 1 side with melted margarine. Place on baking sheet and bake until golden 5 to 8 minutes. Remove from oven; rub margarine-side of bread with cut side of garlic. Set bread aside.

Spread each baguette slice with about 1/2 tsp (2 mL) goat cheese to help red pepper mixture stick to baguette. Using your fingers, pinch a small amount of the red pepper mixture and stick to the goat cheese.

TIME SAVER TIP: Use bottled roasted red peppers. Rinse, drain well, pat dry and cut into bite-sized strips.

Roasted Garlic and Herb Dip

This yogurt-based dip has the wonderful flavour of roasted garlic and fresh herbs. Serve with assorted crudités (raw vegetables), bread sticks and crackers. Dip will keep well for several days in the refrigerator.

1½ cups	low-fat plain yogurt (1% MF)	375 mL
1	large bulb garlic	1
1 tsp	Becel oil	5 mL
2 tbsp	low-fat mayonnaise	30 mL
Pinch	cayenne pepper	Pinch
¼ cup	finely chopped fresh herbs, such as basil, chives, mint or parsley	50 mL
	Salt and freshly ground black pepper to taste	

Preparation: 10 minutes
Refrigeration Time: 4 hours
Cooking Time: 30 minutes
Makes 1 cup (250 mL)

Line a sieve with a coffee filter or paper towels. Place over a large bowl. Turn yogurt into sieve and cover loosely with plastic wrap. Refrigerate 4 hours but preferably overnight until very thick. You should have about ¾ cup (175 mL). Turn thickened yogurt into a bowl.

Preheat oven to 375°F (190°C). Break garlic into cloves (leaving peel on) and place in a single layer in a baking dish. Drizzle with oil and add about ¼ inch (5 mm) water. Bake, uncovered and stirring occasionally, until cloves are tender, 20 to 30 minutes. Squeeze garlic to remove purée; mash.

Stir mashed garlic into thickened yogurt along with mayonnaise, cayenne, herbs, salt and pepper. Cover and refrigerate until serving or overnight. Serve with assorted vegetables and bread sticks.

PRESENTATION TIP: For a special occasion, serve dip in a hollowed-out sweet red or yellow pepper in the centre of a platter surrounded by your favourite raw vegetables.

Nutrients per serving
(1 tbsp/15 mL)
Calories 24
Protein 1.3 g
Fat 1.1 g
  PUFA 0.3 g
  MUFA 0.5 g
  SFA 0.2 g
Carbohydrates 2.5 g
Fibre 0.1 g
Cholesterol 1 mg
Sodium 29 mg
Potassium 65 mg

Mushroom and Fontina Pita Melts

A variety of mushrooms will give an interesting flavour and texture to these simple make-ahead appetizers. The perfect accent is the topping of Fontina cheese, a soft sweet cheese from northern Italy.

Preparation: 25 minutes
Cooking Time: 14 to 18 minutes
Makes 20 appetizers

3 tsp	Becel margarine, regular or salt free, divided	15 mL
1	small onion, chopped	1
1	clove garlic, minced	1
1/2 lb	white mushrooms, thinly sliced	250 g
1/4 lb	shiitake mushrooms, stems removed, thinly sliced	125 g
1 1/2 tsp	chopped fresh thyme (or 1/2 tsp/2 mL dried)	7 mL
1 tbsp	balsamic vinegar or brandy	15 mL
1/4 tsp	salt	1 mL
10	mini pitas, split horizontally in half	10
3/4 cup	shredded Fontina cheese	175 mL
	Fresh thyme or parsley sprigs for garnish	

Nutrients per serving
(1 piece)
Calories 38
Protein 1.7 g
Fat 2 g
  PUFA 0.3 g
  MUFA 0.6 g
  SFA 0.9 g
Carbohydrates 3.5 g
Fibre 0.4 g
Cholesterol 5 mg
Sodium 89 mg
Potassium 53 mg

Preheat oven to 450°F (230°C).

In a large nonstick skillet, melt 1 tsp (5 mL) of the margarine over medium-high heat. Sauté onion and garlic 2 minutes.

Add remaining margarine and stir in mushrooms and thyme; sauté, stirring occasionally, 8 to 10 minutes or until mushrooms are browned and liquid evaporates. Stir in balsamic vinegar or brandy and salt; cook 1 minute. (Mixture may be covered and refrigerated for up to 3 days. Bring to room temperature before proceeding.)

Place pitas in a single layer on a baking sheet. Spoon on mushroom mixture and sprinkle with cheese. Bake for 3 to 5 minutes or until hot and cheese melts. Serve warm garnished with thyme or parsley sprigs, if desired.

SUBSTITUTION: Instead of Fontina cheese, try shredded Provolone or partly skimmed mozzarella.

Cheese and Artichoke Tulips

Use wonton wrappers to create simple and attractive shells for this easy-mix cheese and artichoke filling. Wonton wrappers are usually found in the produce section of the supermarket.

40	wonton wrappers (3 inches/7.5 cm square)	40
1	egg white, lightly beaten	1
1 cup	light ricotta cheese	250 mL
1/2 cup	grated 40%-less-fat Parmesan cheese	125 mL
1 tbsp	Dijon mustard	15 mL
1/2 tsp	hot pepper flakes	2 mL
1	can (14 oz/398 mL) artichoke hearts, drained and chopped	1
2	green onions, chopped	2
1 tbsp	Becel margarine, regular, salt free or light, melted	15 mL
	Fresh thyme or parsley sprigs for garnish	

Preparation: 25 minutes
Cooking Time: 15 minutes
Makes 40 appetizers

Preheat oven to 350°F (180°C). Spray mini muffin tins with nonstick cooking spray. Press wonton wrappers into muffin cups; set aside.

In a bowl, combine egg white with ricotta and Parmesan cheeses, Dijon mustard and hot pepper flakes. Stir in chopped artichoke hearts and green onions. Spoon about 1 tbsp (15 mL) of the filling into each cup. Lightly brush edges of wrappers with margarine.

Bake 10 to 15 minutes or until edges of wrappers are lightly browned. Serve warm garnished with a sprig of parsley or thyme, if desired.

SUBSTITUTION: Instead of ricotta cheese, 1 package (250 g) of softened light cream cheese may be used, but fat content will be higher.

MAKE AHEAD TIP: The filling mixture may be prepared ahead and refrigerated. Fill just before baking.

Nutrients per serving
(1 piece)
Calories 41
Protein 2.4 g
Fat 0.9 g
   PUFA 0.2 g
   MUFA 0.3 g
   SFA 0.4 g
Carbohydrates 5.8 g
Fibre 0.5 g
Cholesterol 3 mg
Sodium 105 mg
Potassium 42 mg

Red Pepper Vegetable Rolls

A savoury blend of sautéed veggies and feta cheese. Serve either as an appetizer or as a quick supper.

Preparation: 15 to 20 minutes
Cooking Time: 15 minutes
Makes 8 appetizers or 4 entrées

4	10-inch (24-cm) flour tortillas	4
2 tbsp	Becel margarine, divided	30 mL
1	medium onion, finely chopped	1
1	clove garlic, minced	1
2	small Italian eggplants (about ½ lb/250 g), chopped	2
½ lb	white mushrooms, thinly sliced	250 g
1	medium sweet red pepper, cut into thin strips	1
¼ cup	crumbled low-fat feta cheese (17.5% MF)	50 mL

DRESSING

1 tbsp	Becel oil	15 mL
1 tbsp	red wine vinegar	15 mL
1 tsp	herbes de Provence*	5 mL
1 tsp	Dijon or sweet honey mustard	5 mL
½ tsp	dried oregano	2 mL
½ tsp	freshly ground black pepper	2 mL
¼ tsp	salt or to taste	1 mL

* or use total of 1½ tsp (7 mL) dried oregano and omit herbes de Provence.

Nutrients per serving (1 roll):
Calories 173
Protein 4.4 g
Fat 7.9 g
  PUFA 2.8 g
  MUFA 3.1 g
  SFA 1.7 g
Carbohydrates 21.8 g
Fibre 2.7 g
Cholesterol 3 mg
Sodium 267 mg
Potassium 247 mg
Good source of vitamin C, thiamine and iron.

Preheat oven to 250°F (120°C). Spread 1 tbsp (15 mL) of the margarine evenly onto all of the tortillas. Wrap tortillas in foil; warm in oven for 10 minutes.

In a large nonstick skillet over medium heat, melt remaining margarine. Sauté onion until softened, about 7 minutes. Add garlic, eggplant and mushrooms. Stir over medium heat for 10 minutes; add peppers and cook 5 minutes more.

In a jar with screwtop lid, measure the dressing ingredients. Replace lid and shake well. Season to taste.

Spread a quarter of the vegetable mixture onto each tortilla, leaving a 1-inch (2.5-cm) border around the edge. Drizzle a quarter of the dressing

Appetizers and Snacks

over each vegetable mound. Top each with 1 tbsp (15 mL) of the feta cheese. Starting from one edge, roll tortillas up firmly. Slice each tortilla in half and secure with a toothpick. Serve immediately.

SUBSTITUTIONS

- Use low-fat cream cheese in place of feta cheese. Spread 1 tbsp (15 mL) onto each tortilla before spooning on the vegetable mixture.
- Zucchini can be substituted for the eggplant.

KITCHEN TIP: Make a double batch of the dressing and use the remainder in a salad.

Herbes de Provence is a mixture of equal amounts of dried herbs such as basil, thyme, sage, rosemary, savory, marjoram, crushed bay leaves and lavender.

Zesty Bean Dip or Spread (Hummus)

Beans are an excellent source of fibre. This tantalizing dip or spread is lower in fat than recipes that use tahini (sesame seed paste). It can be scooped up with crackers or dipped into with raw vegetables such as celery and carrot sticks, sweet pepper slices and zucchini rounds.

Preparation: 10 minutes
Makes 1½ cups (375 mL)

2	cloves garlic, peeled	2
1	can (19 oz/540 mL) white kidney beans, drained and rinsed	1
1 tbsp	Becel oil	15 mL
1 tbsp	lemon juice	15 mL
¼ tsp	*each:* salt, cumin, paprika	1 mL
	Paprika and chopped fresh parsley for garnish	
	Tortilla Crisps (page 41)	

Nutrients per serving
(1 tbsp / 15mL)
Calories 24
Protein 1.3 g
Fat 0.6 g
  PUFA 0.3 g
  MUFA 0.3 g
  SFA 0.1 g
Carbohydrates 3.4 g
Fibre 1.4 g
Cholesterol 0 mg
Sodium 76 mg
Potassium 41 mg

In a food processor, mince garlic. Add kidney beans, oil, lemon juice, salt, cumin and paprika. Process until smooth. For a less thick dipping consistency, blend in a little water.(Dip may be made up to 2 days ahead.)

Spread bean mixture onto a large plate or spoon into a shallow bowl. Garnish edge with parsley and sprinkle lightly with paprika. Serve at room temperature.

SUBSTITUTIONS
- Substitute white pea beans, black beans or chick-peas for the white kidney beans (sometimes labelled cannellini beans).
- Top with chopped sun-dried tomatoes and toasted pine nuts.
- Substitute chopped fresh coriander for the parsley.

Tortilla Crisps

These quick-to-make crisps are ideal with Zesty Bean Dip or other dips.

4	large flour tortillas (any flavour)	4
2 tsp	(approx.) Becel oil	10 mL

Preheat oven to 375°F (190°C). Lightly brush both sides of each tortilla with a little oil. Cut each tortilla into 8 wedges; place in single layer on a baking sheet.

Bake for 6 to 8 minutes, turning once, until crisp. Let cool. Store in tightly covered container for up to 1 day. Re-crisp in a warm oven if necessary.

Preparation: 5 minutes
Cooking Time: 6 to 8 minutes

Nutrients per serving (per crisp)
Calories 26
Protein 0.6 g
Fat 0.8 g
  PUFA 0.3 g
  MUFA 0.3 g
  SFA 0.1 g
Carbohydrates 3.9 g
Fibre 0.2 g
Cholesterol 0 mg
Sodium 34 mg
Potassium 9 mg

Broccoli Lemon Appetizers

Lemony broccoli teamed with olives and capers—tasty as a light appetizer or as a salad.

Preparation: 10 to 15 minutes

Cooking Time:
appetizer—5 minutes,
pita—15 minutes,
homemade Melba toast—
30 minutes

Makes 12 1/2-cup (125-mL) servings

6 cups	broccoli florets	1.5 L
2 tbsp	Becel oil	30 mL
1 tsp	grated lemon rind	5 mL
1 tbsp	lemon juice	15 mL
1/4 tsp	pepper	1 mL
1/2 cup	pitted dry cured olives	125 mL
1 tbsp	capers	15 mL
4	small whole wheat pitas	4
	Salt and freshly ground black pepper to taste	

Nutrients per serving
(Broccoli Lemon
Appetizers only)
Calories 88
Protein 2.8 g
Fat 3.2 g
  PUFA 1.2 g
  MUFA 1.6 g
  SFA 0.4 g
Carbohydrates 12.7 g
Fibre 2.3 g
Cholesterol 0 mg
Sodium 180 mg
Potassium 96 mg
Good source of vitamin C.

Boil or steam broccoli florets just until crisp. Drain well.

In a large bowl, whisk together oil, rind, lemon juice and pepper. Gently stir broccoli into dressing to thoroughly incorporate. Add the olives and capers. Refrigerate for at least 1 hour.

Meanwhile, preheat oven to 250°F (120°C). Cut each pita into 6 wedges. Place on a baking sheet. Bake for 10 to 15 minutes or until crisp. Cool on a rack. Makes 24 triangles.

Season broccoli mixture with salt and pepper before serving. Serve with pita or Melba toast.

Capers are the small closed green flower buds of the caper bush that grows along the shores of the Mediterranean. Capers are salted and pickled and typically used in Mediterranean cooking (in salads, in sauces for chicken, game and fish and in tomato sauces and pizzas). They are available in the condiment section at most grocery stores.

Homemade Melba Toast Trim the crusts off 6 slices of thinly sliced whole wheat bread. Cut each slice into 4 squares. Place on baking sheet. Bake in a preheated 250°F (120°C) oven for 30 minutes. Cool on a rack. Store in an airtight container. Makes 24 squares.

Stuffed Portobello Mushrooms

This appetizer makes an excellent starter for a sit-down dinner. For a meatless version, omit the prosciutto and add 1/2 cup (125 mL) diced sweet red or green pepper.

4	portobello mushrooms (about 4 inches/	
	10 cm wide)	4
3 tsp	Becel oil, divided	15 mL
1/2 cup	diced onion	125 mL
1	clove garlic, minced	1
2 oz	prosciutto, diced	50 g
1/2 tsp	dried thyme (or 1 1/2 tsp/7 mL chopped fresh)	2 mL
	Salt and freshly ground black pepper to taste	
2 tbsp	finely chopped fresh parsley	30 mL
1/4 cup	flaked or thinly sliced Parmesan cheese	50 mL

Preparation: 20 minutes
Cooking Time: 10 minutes
Serves: 4

Preheat oven to 425°F (220°C).

Clean mushrooms; trim stems from caps. Discard stem bottoms; dice stems and reserve. Brush top of caps with 2 tsp (10 mL) of the oil. Place stem side up on a baking sheet or in a baking pan.

Heat remaining 1 tsp (5 mL) oil in large nonstick skillet over medium-high heat. Add onion and sauté 5 minutes. Stir in garlic, prosciutto, thyme and diced mushroom stems. Sauté 2 minutes more. Remove from heat. Season with salt and pepper and stir in parsley.

Fill mushroom caps with mixture. Top with Parmesan cheese. Bake for 10 minutes or until mushroom caps are soft and cheese is melted. Serve immediately.

MAKE AHEAD TIP: This recipe may be prepared ahead and refrigerated for up to 1 day. It will take about 2 minutes longer to cook when cold from refrigerator.

Nutrients per serving
Calories 132
Protein 8.9 g
Fat 7.1 g
    PUFA 1.9 g
    MUFA 2.6 g
    SFA 2.0 g
Carbohydrates 10.7 g
Fibre 3.8 g
Cholesterol 12 mg
Sodium 302 mg
Potassium 647 mg
Excellent source of
    riboflavin, niacin and
    pantothenic acid.

Chunky Vegetable Antipasto

Colourful Italian vegetables are cooked until thick and mellow, and then served as an appetizer on crackers. May be prepared ahead and refrigerated for easy entertaining. Eggplant may be peeled or not, depending on preference.

Preparation: 20 minutes
Cooking Time: 40 minutes
Makes 4 cups (1 L)

1 lb	eggplant	500 g
1 tbsp	Becel light margarine	15 mL
2	large onions, chopped	2
2	cloves garlic, minced	2
2	stalks celery, sliced	2
1	sweet green pepper, diced	1
1	sweet red pepper, diced	1
1/4 cup	chopped fresh parsley	50 mL
1	can (28 oz/796 mL) diced tomatoes	1
2	medium zucchini, chopped	2
3 tbsp	red wine vinegar	45 mL
1 tbsp	granulated sugar	15 mL
1 1/2 tsp	dried basil (or 3 tbsp/45 mL chopped fresh)	7 mL
	Salt and freshly ground black pepper to taste	

Nutrients per 1 tbsp
(15mL)
Calories 10
Protein 0.3 g
Fat 0.1 g
   PUFA 0.1 g
   MUFA 0 g
   SFA 0 g
Carbohydrates 2.1 g
Fibre 0.5 g
Cholesterol 0 mg
Sodium 23 mg
Potassium 75 mg

Preheat broiler. Cut eggplant crosswise into 1-inch (2.5-cm) slices and place on a greased rack on a baking sheet. Broil until lightly browned, turning once, 8 to 10 minutes. Cut into small cubes.

In a large saucepan, melt margarine over medium heat. Cook onions and garlic until soft, about 3 minutes. Add eggplant, celery, green and red peppers and parsley. Cook, stirring often, for 15 minutes.

Stir in tomatoes and their juice, zucchini, vinegar, sugar, basil, salt and pepper. Cook, uncovered, stirring often, until mixture is thick, 20 to 30 minutes. Cool. Best served at room temperature. Serve with crackers.

SERVING SUGGESTION: Choose low-fat crackers to complement the flavours in the antipasto.

Toasted Mushroom Roll-ups

Tasty morsels of bread stuffed with a delectable mixture of herbs, cream cheese and colourful vegetables.

3 tbsp	Becel light margarine, divided	45 mL
1/2 lb	mushrooms, finely chopped	250 g
1	medium onion, finely chopped	1
1/3 cup	finely chopped sweet red or green pepper	75 mL
1	clove garlic, minced	1
1	125-g pkg light cream cheese, softened	1
1/2 tsp	dried basil (or 1 1/2 tsp/7 mL chopped fresh)	2 mL
	Salt and freshly ground black pepper	
16	slices whole wheat sandwich bread, crusts removed	16

Preparation: 20 minutes
Cooking Time: 20 minutes
Makes 48 appetizers

In a large skillet, heat 1 tbsp (15 mL) of the margarine over medium heat. Add mushrooms, onion and sweet pepper; sauté for 5 minutes or until tender. Add garlic; sauté 1 minute more. Remove from heat. Stir in cheese and basil until smooth. Season to taste with salt and pepper. Set aside.

Roll slices of bread lightly with a rolling pin to flatten. Spread about 2 tbsp (30 mL) of the filling on each slice. Roll up tightly; fasten with toothpick. Place seam side down on a baking sheet. Cover with plastic wrap and chill for 1 hour. (Roll-ups may be frozen for up to 2 weeks. Defrost 30 minutes before baking.)

Melt the remaining 2 tbsp (30 mL) of margarine. Brush over bread rolls. Bake at 400°F (200°C) for 15 to 20 minutes or until golden. Remove toothpicks; cut each roll into 3 pieces. Serve hot.

Nutrients per roll-up
Calories 31
Protein 0.9 g
Fat 1.1 g
PUFA 0.2 g
MUFA 0.4 g
SFA 0.4 g
Carbohydrates 4.3 g
Fibre 0.2 g
Cholesterol 2 mg
Sodium 55 mg
Potassium 28 mg

Soups

Fast

When You Have More Time

White Bean Soup with Red Pepper Purée

This hearty soup is great for any occasion, but adding the red pepper purée makes an elegant addition for entertaining. Either use purchased roasted red peppers or roast your own following the easy directions below.

2 tsp	Becel margarine, regular or salt free	10 mL
1	medium onion, chopped	1
2	cloves garlic, minced	2
1/2 cup	*each:* chopped carrots and celery	125 mL
2 1/2 cups	sodium-reduced chicken broth	625 mL
1	can (19 oz/540 mL) white kidney beans, drained and rinsed	1
1/2 tsp	dried thyme (or 1 1/2 tsp/7 mL chopped fresh)	2 mL
Pinch	freshly ground black pepper	Pinch
1/4 cup	red pepper purée (see Kitchen Tips)	50 mL
1 tbsp	fat-free sour cream or yogurt	15 mL

Preparation: 15 minutes
Cooking Time: 20 minutes
Serves: 4

In a large saucepan or Dutch oven, melt margarine over medium heat. Sauté onion, garlic, carrots and celery for 5 minutes.

Stir in chicken broth, kidney beans, thyme and pepper. Bring to a boil. Cover and simmer 15 minutes or until vegetables are tender.

In blender or food processor, purée soup in batches until smooth. Return to saucepan and heat through.

Stir together red pepper purée and sour cream or yogurt. Spoon soup into bowls and top with about 1 tbsp (15 mL) red pepper purée; use a knife to swirl it though the soup.

Nutrients per serving
Calories 179
Protein 11.8 g
Fat 3.3 g
  PUFA 1.2 g
  MUFA 1.2 g
  SFA 0.6 g
Carbohydrates 26.3 g
Fibre 9.3 g
Cholesterol 0 mg
Sodium 837 mg
Potassium 505 mg
Excellent source of vitamin A and folacin. Contains a very high amount of dietary fibre.

- Roasted red peppers are available in jars in supermarkets. Drain peppers and blot dry with paper towel. To purée, place large roasted red peppers in food processor or blender and process until smooth.
- To roast your own red peppers: Cut in half lengthwise and remove seeds. Place cut side down on broiler pan or baking sheet. Broil until skin is blackened, 5 to 8 minutes. Remove from oven and place in bag or covered dish to steam for 15 minutes. Remove skins with paring knife. Refrigerate for up to 1 week or freeze for longer storage.

SERVING SUGGESTION: Serve with a tossed green salad and crusty bread for a balanced meal.

Tuscan-style Spinach and Bean Soup

Who says you can't make soup quickly? This hearty, thick soup is ready in no time at all and is bursting with nutrition.

1 tbsp	Becel margarine	15 mL
1	medium onion, chopped	1
2	cloves garlic, minced	2
1	large carrot, peeled and diced	1
3 cups	sodium-reduced chicken broth	750 mL
1	can (28 oz/796 mL) diced tomatoes	1
1½ tsp	dried oregano (or 1½ tbsp/20 mL chopped fresh)	7 mL
½ tsp	dried basil (or 1½ tsp/7 mL chopped fresh)	2 mL
1	can (19 oz/540 mL) white kidney beans, drained and rinsed	1
1	pkg (10 oz/284 g) spinach, trimmed, washed and coarsely chopped	1
	Freshly ground black pepper	
¼ cup	grated Parmesan cheese	50 mL
	Chopped fresh basil for garnish	

Preparation: 20 minutes
Cooking Time: 35 minutes
Serves: 6

In a large saucepan or Dutch oven, melt margarine over medium heat. Add onion, garlic and carrot; cook gently, stirring occasionally, for 5 minutes. Add chicken broth, diced tomatoes, oregano and basil. Bring to a boil, reduce heat and simmer, uncovered, for 10 minutes.

Stir in beans. Bring soup to a boil. Stir in spinach; cook on medium heat for 1 minute. If soup is too thick, add a little extra chicken broth or water. Season with pepper to taste. Serve sprinkled with Parmesan cheese and garnish with chopped fresh basil.

Nutrients per serving
Calories 168
Protein 8.9 g
Fat 6 g
  PUFA 1.8 g
  MUFA 2 g
  SFA 1.4 g
Carbohydrates 20.7 g
Fibre 7.2 g
Cholesterol 3 mg
Sodium 795 mg
Potassium 732 mg
Excellent source of vitamin A, folacin and magnesium. Contains a very high amount of dietary fibre.

Zucchini Basil Soup

This light and refreshing soup is a favourite in the summer when zucchini and fresh basil are both plentiful, but it is enjoyable year-round.

Preparation: 15 minutes
Cooking Time: about 25 minutes
Serves: 4

1 tbsp	Becel margarine	15 mL
1	medium onion, chopped	1
2	cloves garlic, minced	2
5	medium zucchini, chopped (about 7 to 8 cups/1.75 to 2 L)	5
4 cups	sodium-reduced chicken broth	1 L
1 tbsp	lemon juice	15 mL
2 tsp	granulated sugar	10 mL
1/3 cup	chopped fresh basil	75 mL
4 tbsp	non-fat plain yogurt	60 mL
	Salt and freshly ground black pepper	
	Basil sprigs and paprika for garnish	

Nutrients per serving
Calories 125
Protein 7.5 g
Fat 4.3 g
    PUFA 1.5 g
    MUFA 1.7 g
    SFA 0.8 g
Carbohydrates 15 g
Fibre 3.7 g
Cholesterol 0 mg
Sodium 820 mg
Potassium 811 mg
Good source of niacin, folacin, vitamin B12 and magnesium.

In a large saucepan or Dutch oven, melt margarine over medium heat. Add onion and cook, stirring often, for 7 minutes or until softened. Add garlic and zucchini and cook, stirring occasionally, for 3 minutes. Stir in chicken broth, lemon juice and sugar. Bring to a boil, reduce heat and simmer, uncovered, for 15 minutes or until zucchini is tender. Stir in basil; simmer for 1 minute more.

In a blender or food processor, purée soup in batches until smooth. Return to saucepan and reheat. Season to taste with salt and pepper. Spoon into serving bowls. Add 1 tbsp (15 mL) yogurt in the centre of each; garnish with a sprig of basil and a sprinkle of paprika.

TIME SAVER TIP: Use a food processor to shred the zucchini and save preparation and cooking time.

Southwestern Fennel and Corn Soup

Here's an easy way to try a new vegetable. This puréed vegetable soup features fennel and is topped with a wonderful sour cream and sun-dried tomato garnish.

1	bulb fennel, about 1 lb (500 g)	1
2 tsp	Becel margarine	10 mL
1	medium onion, chopped	1
1	small carrot, sliced	1
2	cloves garlic, minced	2
2¹/₂ to 3 cups	chicken or vegetable broth	625 to 750 mL
¹/₂ cup	fresh or frozen corn	125 mL
1 tsp	dried oregano (or 1 tbsp/15 mL chopped fresh)	5 mL
¹/₂ tsp	chili powder	2 mL
	Salt and freshly ground black pepper	
¹/₄ cup	light sour cream (5% MF)	50 mL
2 tbsp	chopped drained oil-packed sun-dried tomatoes	30 mL

Preparation: 10 minutes
Cooking Time: 20 minutes
Serves: 4

Remove fronds from fennel, saving some for garnish. Remove core from fennel. Coarsely chop remaining fennel. In a large saucepan, heat margarine over medium heat. Add onion, carrot and garlic; cook, stirring frequently, for 3 minutes. Add fennel, 2¹/₂ cups (625 mL) chicken or vegetable broth, corn, oregano and chili powder. Cover, bring to a boil, then simmer and cook until fennel is very tender, 20 to 25 minutes. Add salt and pepper to taste.

In a food processor, purée fennel mixture until smooth (soup will have texture). If necessary, thin with additional chicken or vegetable broth. Ladle soup into serving bowls. Top with sour cream and swirl through soup. Garnish with fennel fronds and sun-dried tomatoes.

Nutrients per serving:
Calories 137
Protein 6.7 g
Fat 4.4 g
  PUFA 1.2 g
  MUFA 1.7 g
  SFA 1.0 g
Carbohydrates 19 g
Fibre 5.1 g
Cholesterol 2 mg
Sodium 598 mg
Potassium 794 mg
Excellent source of vitamin A. Good source of niacin and folacin. Contains high amount of dietary fibre.

> **Fennel** is an aromatic plant that has a broad bulb-shaped base, pale green celery-like stems and bright green feathery foliage. It has a light anise flavour that is strongest when raw and becomes even milder when cooked. It is rich in vitamin A and contains a fair amount of calcium, phosphorus and potassium. Fennel may be used raw in salads or cooked in a variety of ways such as braising or sautéing or in soups. It is available from fall through spring. When buying fennel, choose one that has a gentle licorice aroma, is firm to the touch, pale green and free of blemishes. The fronds should appear fresh, not wilted.

A Mexican Gathering

Invite your friends over for a fun evening and introduce them to a little light-hearted Mexican food! Prepare the soup ahead of time and put all the fixings for the fajitas on the table so everyone can help themselves.

Zesty Bean Dip or Spread (page 40)
Southwestern Fennel and Corn Soup (page 51)
Chicken Fajitas (page 100)
Fresh Fruit Salad and Cranberry Dressing (page 66)

Creamy Sweet Potato and Parsnip Soup

Here's a creamy soup without the cream! The flavours of the sweet potatoes and parsnips blend beautifully in this tasty mellow soup.

1 tbsp	Becel margarine	15 mL
1	large onion, chopped	1
2	parsnips, peeled and sliced	2
1½ lb	sweet potatoes (about 2 large), peeled and cut into chunks	750 g
¾ tsp	ground nutmeg	4 mL
¼ tsp	salt	1 mL
4 cups	chicken broth	1 L
1 cup	1% milk	250 mL
1 tbsp	light brown sugar	15 mL
	Salt and freshly ground black pepper to taste	

Preparation: 15 minutes
Cooking Time: 30 minutes
Serves: 4 to 6

In a large saucepan or Dutch oven, melt margarine over medium heat. Add onion and sauté until softened, about 5 minutes. Stir in parsnips and sweet potatoes; sauté for 2 minutes more. Season with nutmeg and salt.

Stir in chicken broth and bring to a boil. Reduce heat to low and simmer gently, partially covered, for 30 minutes or until vegetables are tender.

In a blender or food processor, purée soup in batches until smooth. Return soup to saucepan, stir in milk and heat to serving temperature. Do not allow the soup to boil. Stir in brown sugar. Season to taste with salt and pepper.

SUBSTITUTION: Instead of chicken broth, use vegetable stock or water.

Nutrients per serving
Calories 221
Protein 7.2 g
Fat 3.8 g
 PUFA 1.1 g
 MUFA 1.4 g
 SFA 1 g
Carbohydrates 40 g
Fibre 4.3 g
Cholesterol 2 mg
Sodium 670 mg
Potassium 597 mg
Excellent source of vitamin A. Contains a high amount of dietary fibre.

Potato and Leek Soup

A rich and satisfying soup without a lot of fat. For lunch, serve with a crisp green salad and some good crusty bread. For dinner, stir in some diced cooked chicken or ham.

Preparation: 15 minutes
Cooking Time: 20 minutes
Serves: 4

2 tbsp	Becel margarine	30 mL
3	medium leeks (white part only), sliced	3
1½ cups	sodium-reduced chicken broth	375 mL
3	medium potatoes, peeled and diced	3
3	medium carrots, sliced	3
½ tsp	dried marjoram (or 1½ tsp/7 mL chopped fresh)	2 mL
½ tsp	dried thyme (or 1½ tsp/7 mL chopped fresh)	2 mL
¼ tsp	freshly ground black pepper	1 mL
2 tbsp	all-purpose flour	30 mL
2 cups	skim milk	500 mL
	Chopped fresh parsley for garnish	

Nutrients per serving
Calories 254
Protein 7.8 g
Fat 6.4 g
  PUFA 2.5 g
  MUFA 2.3 g
  SFA 1.0 g
Carbohydrates 43 g
Fibre 5.2 g
Cholesterol 2 mg
Sodium 410 mg
Potassium 750 mg
Excellent source of vitamin A, vitamin B6, vitamin B12. Contains a high amount of dietary fibre.

In a large saucepan or Dutch oven, melt margarine over medium heat. Add leeks and sauté for 3 to 5 minutes or until tender. Add chicken broth, potatoes, carrots, marjoram, thyme and pepper. Cover, bring to a boil, then reduce heat and simmer for 10 minutes or until vegetables are tender.

Dissolve flour in milk. Stir into soup and cook, stirring occasionally, until soup is thickened and bubbly. Spoon into bowls and sprinkle with chopped parsley.

Minestrone

Here's a quick and hearty vegetable soup with a touch of herbs. Serve with thick slices of whole grain bread for a satisfying dinner.

2 tbsp	Becel margarine	30 mL
1	large onion, chopped	1
2	cloves garlic, minced	2
1	medium zucchini, quartered lengthwise and sliced	1
6 cups	chicken or vegetable broth	1.5 L
1	can (19 oz/540 mL) diced tomatoes	1
1	can (19 oz/540 mL) mixed beans, drained and rinsed (or 2 cups/500 mL cooked beans)	1
2 cups	fresh or frozen green beans	500 mL
1½ tsp	dried basil (or 1½ tbsp/20 mL chopped fresh)	7 mL
½ tsp	dried oregano (or 1½ tsp/7 mL chopped fresh)	2 mL
⅓ cup	orzo or small soup pasta	75 mL
⅓ cup	chopped fresh parsley	75 mL
	Salt and freshly ground black pepper to taste	
6 tbsp	grated Parmesan cheese	90 mL

Preparation: 15 minutes
Cooking Time: 25 minutes
Serves: 6

In a large saucepan or Dutch oven, melt margarine over medium heat. Add onion and cook, stirring often, for 7 minutes or until softened. Stir in garlic and zucchini; cook, stirring often, for 3 minutes. Stir in chicken or vegetable broth, tomatoes, mixed beans, green beans, and basil and oregano (if using dried). Bring to a boil, cover and simmer 5 minutes.

Stir in orzo; reduce heat, cover and simmer 5 minutes. Stir in parsley, basil and oregano (if using fresh). Season to taste with salt and pepper. Serve with 1 tbsp (15 mL) Parmesan cheese sprinkled over each serving.

SUBSTITUTION: Substitute mixed beans with Romano, kidney or other beans.

Nutrients per serving
Calories 212
Protein 12.7 g
Fat 7.5 g
  PUFA 2.1 g
  MUFA 2.7 g
  SFA 2.1 g
Carbohydrates 24.4 g
Fibre 5.8 g
Cholesterol 5 mg
Sodium 1235 mg
Potassium 692 mg
Excellent source of niacin.
  Contains high amount of
  dietary fibre.

Gazpacho

On a warm summer's evening what could be more delicious than this refreshing cold soup, full of crunchy vegetables? For a change, top it with a spoonful of light yogurt or sour cream and sprinkle with finely chopped fresh chives or basil.

Preparation: 30 minutes
Cooking Time:
  soup—9 minutes,
  croutons—30 minutes
Makes 10 1-cup (250-mL)
  servings

1 tbsp	Becel margarine	15 mL
1	medium onion, finely chopped	1
2	cloves garlic, minced	2
1/2 tsp	dried basil (or 1 1/2 tsp/7 mL chopped fresh)	2 mL
1	seedless cucumber, diced	1
1	*each:* medium sweet red, green and yellow pepper, diced	1
2	stalks celery, finely chopped	2
1	can (48 oz/1.36 L) tomato or vegetable cocktail juice	1
3 tbsp	red wine vinegar	45 mL
1 tbsp	Becel oil	15 mL
1 tbsp	Worcestershire sauce	15 mL
	Salt to taste	
1/2 tsp	freshly ground black pepper	2 mL
1 tbsp	finely chopped chives or green onion tops	15 mL

Nutrients per serving
Calories 67
Protein 2 g
Fat 2.6 g
  PUFA 1.1 g
  MUFA 1.1 g
  SFA 0.3 g
Carbohydrates 11 g
Fibre 2 g
Cholesterol 0 mg
Sodium 528 mg
Potassium 471 mg
Excellent source of vitamin
  C. Good source of
  vitamin A, vitamin B6
  and folacin.

In a frying pan, melt margarine over medium heat; add onion and sauté for 7 minutes or until softened. Add garlic and basil; cook for another 2 minutes.

Transfer onion mixture to a food processor or blender. Add half of the cucumber, half of the sweet peppers and half of the celery. Add 1 cup (250 mL) of the tomato juice and process until smooth. Transfer mixture to a large bowl and stir in the remaining prepared vegetables, remaining tomato juice, vinegar, oil and Worcestershire sauce.

Refrigerate for at least 3 hours or preferably overnight. Season with salt and pepper. Garnish with chopped chives or green onions. Serve with oven-toasted croutons.

> **Oven-toasted Croutons** Trim crusts off 4 slices of whole wheat bread. Cut bread into small cubes. Bake in a preheated 250°F (120°C) oven for 30 minutes. Cool on cooling rack before storing in airtight container.

Alfresco Summer Meal

Here's a tasty menu for a hot summer's evening. This menu works particularly well during high summer when vegetables and strawberries are at their peak. Prepare the Gazpacho and salad ahead of time so you can spend more time at the table. Assemble the shortcakes just before serving.

Gazpacho (page 57)
Lime and Ginger Grilled Salmon (page 118)
Tropical Rice (page 138)
Crunchy Vegetable Summer Salad (page 72)
Strawberry Almond Shortcakes (page 154)

Hearty Italian Tomato Soup

A thick and chunky soup that sticks to your ribs—just what you crave on a frosty evening. For a vegetarian version, substitute vegetable broth for beef broth.

Preparation: 20 minutes
Cooking Time: 45 minutes
Serves: 6 to 8

1 tbsp	Becel margarine	15 mL
1	large onion, chopped	1
2	stalks celery, sliced	2
2	medium carrots, chopped	2
2	cloves garlic, minced	2
1	can (28 oz/796 mL) crushed tomatoes	1
6 cups	sodium-reduced beef broth	1.5 L
1½ cups	shredded cabbage	375 mL
1½ tsp	*each:* dried basil leaves and oregano (or 1½ tbsp/20 mL each chopped fresh)	7 mL
1 cup	small pasta shells, elbow macaroni or bow tie pasta	250 mL
1	can (19 oz/540 mL) kidney beans (red or white), chick-peas or black beans, drained and rinsed	1
½ cup	chopped fresh parsley	125 mL
	Grated Parmesan cheese for garnish	

Nutrients per serving
Calories 239
Protein 12.1 g
Fat 3.2 g
  PUFA 1.2 g
  MUFA 0.9 g
  SFA 0.4 g
Carbohydrates 44.7 g
Fibre 10.5 g
Cholesterol 0 mg
Sodium 940 mg
Potassium 1009 mg
Excellent source of vitamin A, folacin, magnesium and iron. Contains a very high amount of dietary fibre.

In a large saucepan or Dutch oven over medium heat, cook onion, celery, carrots and garlic in margarine for 10 minutes, stirring frequently.

Add tomatoes, beef broth, cabbage, basil and oregano (if using dried). Bring to a boil; reduce heat, cover and simmer for 15 minutes.

Stir in pasta and beans. Cook for 20 minutes longer, stirring often. Stir in parsley (and fresh basil and oregano, if using). Serve sprinkled with grated Parmesan cheese.

NUTRITION TIP: A soup with beans and vegetables can easily replace the traditional meat-and-potatoes meal.

Ruby Red Borscht

Not only is this soup full of mellow flavour and colour, it's good for you too!
And it's very easy to make when you use canned beets.

1 tbsp	Becel oil	15 mL
1	medium onion, sliced	1
2	cloves garlic, minced	2
1 tsp	cumin seed	5 mL
2 cups	finely chopped cabbage	500 mL
1	medium potato, peeled and grated	1
3 cups	sodium-reduced beef broth	750 mL
2	cans (each 14 oz/398 mL) sliced beets, drained and cubed; reserve liquid	2
2 tbsp	red wine vinegar	30 mL
1/4 to 1/2 tsp	freshly ground black pepper	1 to 2 mL

GARNISH

1 tbsp	chopped fresh dill	15 mL
1/3 cup	fat-free sour cream	75 mL

Preparation: 20 minutes
Cooking Time: 35 minutes
Serves: 6

In a large saucepan or Dutch oven, heat oil over medium-high heat. Add onion and sauté until softened, about 5 minutes. Add garlic, cumin seed, cabbage and potato. Cook, stirring, for 2 minutes. Add beef broth, beets, reserved beet juice, vinegar and pepper. Bring to a boil; reduce heat and simmer, partially covered, for 30 to 35 minutes or until vegetables are tender. Garnish with sour cream and dill.

Nutrients per serving
Calories 112
Protein 3.5 g
Fat 2.5 g
  PUFA 1.1 g
  MUFA 1.0 g
  SFA 0.2 g
Carbohydrates 20.4 g
Fibre 2.6 g
Cholesterol 0 mg
Sodium 692 mg
Potassium 404 mg
Good source of folacin.
  Contains a moderate
  amount of dietary fibre.

Simmering Seafood Soup

Halibut and shrimp are simmered in a delicious tomato clam broth for this hearty soup. Serve with a crusty loaf of bread and a green salad.

Preparation: 10 to 15 minutes
Cooking Time: 35 minutes
Serves: 6

1	400-g pkg frozen firm white fish, such as halibut or cod	1
2 tsp	Becel margarine or Becel oil	10 mL
1	medium onion, chopped	1
2	cloves garlic, minced	2
1	can (28 oz/796 mL) diced plum tomatoes	1
1	bottle (240 mL) clam juice	1
1/2 cup	dry white wine or tomato juice	125 mL
4	sprigs fresh thyme, chopped (or 1 tsp/5 mL dried)	4
1 tsp	saffron threads (optional)	5 mL
1/2 lb	peeled uncooked large shrimp	250 g
1/4 cup	chopped fresh parsley	50 mL
	Hot pepper sauce to taste	
	Salt and freshly ground black pepper to taste	

Nutrients per serving
Calories 167
Protein 23.3 g
Fat 3.8 g
  PUFA 1.5 g
  MUFA 1.1 g
  SFA 0.6 g
Carbohydrates 8.5 g
Fibre 1.8 g
Cholesterol 80 mg
Sodium 411 mg
Potassium 761 mg
Excellent source of niacin, vitamin B12 and magnesium.

Let fish thaw for 15 minutes at room temperature, then cut into bite-sized chunks. Meanwhile, in a large saucepan or Dutch oven, melt margarine over medium heat. Add onion and garlic; cook until just soft, about 3 minutes. Add tomatoes and their juice, clam juice, white wine or tomato juice, thyme and saffron (if using). Bring mixture to a boil and simmer, covered and stirring occasionally, for 15 minutes.

Stir in partially frozen fish; cook 3 minutes. Stir in shrimp and continue to cook, stirring occasionally, until shrimp and fish are cooked through, about 5 minutes. Stir in parsley. Add hot pepper sauce, salt and pepper to taste.

KITCHEN TIP: Fish may be defrosted in a microwave for a few minutes just until easy enough to cut.

Scallop and Vegetable Soup

A super-easy supper solution that's light and tasty.

2 tbsp	Becel margarine or Becel oil	30 mL
1	onion, sliced	1
2	carrots, julienned	2
2	stalks celery, julienned	2
2	tomatoes, seeded and diced	2
1 cup	sliced mushrooms	250 mL
1 tsp	dried basil (or 1 tbsp/15 mL chopped fresh)	5 mL
1/4 tsp	freshly ground black pepper	1 mL
1	clove garlic, minced	1
2 1/2 cups	chicken broth	625 mL
1/2 lb	fresh or frozen scallops	250 g
1 tbsp	lemon juice	15 mL

Preparation: 15 minutes
Cooking Time: 10 to 15 minutes
Serves: 6

In a large saucepan or Dutch oven, heat margarine or oil over medium-high heat. Add onion, carrots, celery, tomatoes, mushrooms, basil (if using dried) and pepper; sauté until vegetables are tender, 5 to 7 minutes. Add garlic and sauté for 1 minute more.

Add chicken broth, bring to a boil and simmer for 5 minutes. Add scallops, cover and simmer for 5 minutes more or until scallops are tender. Stir in lemon juice and fresh basil (if using) and serve.

SUBSTITUTION: Use 1 tbsp (15 mL) finely chopped fresh dill instead of basil.

Nutrients per serving
Calories 114
Protein 9.6 g
Fat 4.7 g
  PUFA 1.8 g
  MUFA 1.8 g
  SFA 0.7 g
Carbohydrates 8.5 g
Fibre 1.8 g
Cholesterol 12 mg
Sodium 449 mg
Potassium 444 mg
Excellent source of vitamin A. Good source of niacin and vitamin B12.

Hot and Sour Chicken Soup

A warming soup with a good spice level, made easy using the convenience of packaged sliced coleslaw. For a milder taste reduce the amount of hot pepper flakes. Be sure to discard the stems of shiitake mushrooms because they are woody and tough.

Preparation: 10 minutes
Cooking Time: 10 minutes
Serves: 4

2 tsp	Becel oil	10 mL
4 oz	shiitake mushrooms, stems removed, thinly sliced	125 g
2	cloves garlic, minced	2
3 cups	chicken broth	750 mL
2 tbsp	*each:* rice vinegar and light soy sauce	30 mL
2 tsp	minced fresh ginger	10 mL
1/4 tsp	hot pepper flakes	1 mL
2 cups	prepared coleslaw mix (no dressing)	500 mL
1 cup	shredded cooked chicken	250 mL
1 tbsp	*each:* cornstarch and cold water	15 mL

Nutrients per serving
Calories 141
Protein 14.8 g
Fat 6 g
  PUFA 1.8 g
  MUFA 2.3 g
  SFA 1.2 g
Carbohydrates 6.8 g
Fibre 1.1 g
Cholesterol 30 mg
Sodium 914 mg
Potassium 406 mg
Excellent source of niacin.
  Good source of vitamin
  B12.

In a large saucepan or Dutch oven, heat oil over medium-high heat. Sauté mushrooms and garlic, stirring frequently, for 2 minutes.

Add chicken broth, rice vinegar, soy sauce, ginger and hot pepper flakes; bring to a boil. Stir in coleslaw mix and chicken. Cover and simmer 5 minutes.

Dissolve cornstarch in cold water. Stir into soup; simmer 2 minutes or until slightly thickened.

SUBSTITUTIONS
- Instead of shiitake mushrooms, use white mushrooms.
- For a flavour variation, stir in 1/2 tsp (2 mL) sesame oil just before serving.
- Instead of rice vinegar, white vinegar may be used.

Salads

Fast

When You Have More Time

Orange and Beet Salad

This attractive and healthy combination of fruit and vegetables makes a wonderfully delicate salad. Serve individually on salad plates or create a large arrangement on a platter and let everyone help themselves.

Preparation: 15 minutes
Serves: 6

DRESSING

2 tbsp	Becel oil	30 mL
2 tbsp	orange juice	30 mL
1 tbsp	balsamic vinegar or red wine vinegar	15 mL
1 tbsp	Dijon mustard	15 mL
1 tsp	honey	5 mL
1/4 tsp	salt	1 mL

SALAD

4 cups	baby spinach leaves	1 L
4	medium cooked beets, julienned (2 cups/500 mL)	4
2	oranges, peeled and sliced	2
1 cup	thinly sliced cucumber	250 mL

Nutrients per serving
Calories 105
Protein 2.7 g
Fat 4.8 g
  PUFA 2.2 g
  MUFA 2.0 g
  SFA 0.4 g
Carbohydrates 14.8 g
Fibre 3.0 g
Cholesterol 0 mg
Sodium 201 mg
Potassium 498 mg
Excellent source of vitamin A, vitamin C and folacin.

In a small bowl, whisk together dressing ingredients; set aside. (Dressing may be made up to 1 day ahead; refrigerate until needed.)

Arrange cleaned and dried spinach on plates. Top with beets, oranges and cucumber. Drizzle with dressing.

TIME SAVER TIPS

- Use packaged pre-washed baby spinach, or large leaf spinach torn into bite-sized pieces.
- Instead of cooking the beets, use 1 can (14 oz/398 mL) sliced beets, drained and cut into julienne strips. Be sure to chill the beets first for a refreshing salad.

Opposite: Zucchini Basil Soup (page 50)
Overleaf: Cheese and Artichoke Tulips (page 37)

KITCHEN TIP: To cook beets, cut off beet tops, leaving about 1 inch (2.5 cm) of the stem. Scrub gently but do not remove skin. A simple way to cook beets is in the microwave oven. Place in covered casserole with small amount of water; microwave on High for 10 to 12 minutes, stirring once. Or cook beets in a large saucepan of lightly salted boiling water, covered, until tender, 45 to 60 minutes depending on size and age of beets. After cooking, let cool slightly and run under cold water to help remove skins.

Folacin (Folic Acid)

Folic acid is one of the B vitamins. Recent research suggests that folic acid plays an important role in a heart healthy diet

Good food sources of folic acid include: green leafy vegetables, oranges, strawberries, liver, dried beans, peas, enriched grain products.

Opposite: Roasted Garlic and Herb Dip (page 35)
Overleaf: Ginger Carrots and Broccoli with Sesame Seeds (page 132)

Fresh Fruit Salad with Cranberry Dressing

Try this simple low-fat cranberry dressing with these fruit (or use your favourites) or use it with other salads or desserts—use your imagination! It is particularly good with fresh fall fruits like cranberries.

Preparation: 15 minutes
Cooking Time: 4 minutes
Serves: 6

DRESSING

1 1/4 cups	fresh or frozen cranberries	300 mL
1/3 cup	water	75 mL
1/3 cup	granulated sugar	75 mL
1 tbsp	red wine vinegar	15 mL
1 tbsp	becel oil	15 mL
1/4 tsp	salt	1 mL

SALAD

6	Boston lettuce leaves	6
2	kiwis, peeled and sliced	2
2	pears or apples, sliced	2
1	mango, peeled and sliced	1
1/2	pineapple, cut into wedges	1/2
	Fresh mint for garnish	

Nutrients per serving
Calories 162
Protein 1 g
Fat 2.8 g
  PUFA 1.1 g
  MUFA 1.1 g
  SFA 0.2 g
Carbohydrates 36.1 g
Fibre 3.8 g
Cholesterol 0 mg
Sodium 99 mg
Potassium 289 mg
Excellent source of
  vitamin C.

To make the dressing, in a small saucepan combine cranberries and water. Bring to a boil, stirring occasionally. Reduce heat to low, cover and simmer 4 minutes or just until berries begin to pop and soften. Remove from heat and stir in sugar and vinegar. Cool.

Press through sieve and discard skins. Stir in oil and salt. Cover and chill. (May be prepared up to this point 1 day ahead.)

Line salad plates with lettuce and arrange sliced fruit on top. Drizzle with dressing. Garnish with mint.

SUBSTITUTION: **Try different fruit, such as sliced oranges, grapefruit or berries.**

- Salad may be prepared on individual salad plates or on a large platter.
- Serve this salad as a main course by adding sliced cooked chicken or pork.
- This dressing is so good you will find lots of interesting ways to serve it. Try tossing it with berries and serve over frozen yogurt.

MAKE AHEAD TIP: Prepare the fruits ahead; brush pears and apples with lemon juice to prevent browning and store in refrigerator. (Store packaged cranberries in the freezer for use year round.)

Fruit Storage Tips

Knowing how to store fruits and vegetables can help you get the best value for your food dollar. Here are a few handy fruit storage tips:

- Store fruits and vegetables separately in refrigerator. (Fruits produce ethylene gas which cause vegetables to spoil).
- Store apples in a perforated plastic bag for up to 1 month. Apples soften 10 times faster at room temperature.
- Refrigerate up to 2 days unwashed strawberries in a shallow container lined with paper towel.
- Store whole melons at room temperature until ripe. When ripe, store in refrigerator, in a tightly sealed container, away from other produce. Most melons will keep up to 3 days in the refrigerator. Watermelon will keep up to 1 week.
- Store mangoes at room temperature until ripe. When ripe store in refrigerator, covered, for up to 3 days.
- Store whole fresh pineapple in the refrigerator for 2 to 3 days.

Mediterranean Chick-pea and Vegetable Salad

This simple summer salad is a snap to prepare and keeps well, refrigerated, for several days. It's ideal to take for lunch or on a picnic.

Preparation: 15 minutes
Serves: 4 to 6

2 tbsp	Becel oil	30 mL
2 tbsp	lemon juice	30 mL
2 tbsp	orange juice	30 mL
1 1/2 tsp	liquid honey	7 mL
1/2 tsp	ground cumin	2 mL
1/2 tsp	Dijon mustard	2 mL
Pinch	cayenne pepper	Pinch
1	can (19 oz/540 mL) chick-peas, rinsed and drained	1
1	sweet red pepper, cut into thin strips	1
1	medium carrot, sliced	1
3	green onions, sliced	3
1/4 cup	finely chopped fresh coriander or parsley	50 mL
2 tbsp	currants	30 mL
	Salt to taste	

Nutrients per serving
Calories 229
Protein 7.8 g
Fat 8.3 g
  PUFA 3.7 g
  MUFA 3.3 g
  SFA 0.8 g
Carbohydrates 33 g
Fibre 4.5 g
Cholesterol 0 mg
Sodium 225 mg
Potassium 337 mg
Excellent source of vitamin A, vitamin C, vitamin B6 and folacin. Contains a high amount of dietary fibre.

In a small bowl, whisk together oil, lemon juice, orange juice, honey, cumin, mustard and cayenne pepper. Set aside.

In a serving bowl, combine chick-peas, red pepper, carrot, green onions, coriander and currants. Toss with dressing. Add salt to taste. Cover and refrigerate until serving.

Potato, Green Bean and Red Onion Salad

This colourful salad is ideal for a backyard barbecue or picnic and is a wonderful change from the traditional mayonnaise version.

1 lb	potatoes, peeled and cut into bite-sized chunks	500 g
1/3 cup	diced red onion	75 mL
1/4 lb	green beans, trimmed and cut in half	125 g
2 tbsp	Becel oil	30 mL
2 tbsp	white wine vinegar	30 mL
2 tbsp	low-fat plain yogurt (2% MF)	30 mL
2	cloves garlic, minced	2
1/3 cup	chopped fresh mint, basil or parsley	75 mL
	Salt and freshly ground black pepper	

Preparation: 15 minutes
Cooking Time: 6 minutes
Serves: 4 to 6

Place potatoes in a saucepan with water to cover. Cover and bring to a boil, then reduce heat and simmer until tender, 5 to 7 minutes. Drain well and place in a serving bowl with red onion. Bring another saucepan of water to a boil. Add green beans; cook 1 minute. Drain well; rinse under cold running water to stop the cooking. Drain; set aside.

Whisk together oil and vinegar. Toss half the dressing with the hot potatoes and red onion. Let potatoes cool.

Stir yogurt and garlic into remaining vinegar mixture. Toss together potatoes, beans, yogurt mixture and herbs. Season with salt and pepper to taste. Serve immediately or cover and refrigerate until serving.

Nutrients per serving
Calories 154
Protein 2.7 g
Fat 6.8 g
  PUFA 3.1 g
  MUFA 3.0 g
  SFA 0.7 g
Carbohydrates 21.8 g
Fibre 2.3 g
Cholesterol 0 mg
Sodium 12 mg
Potassium 425 mg
Good source of
  vitamin B6.

Mexican Bean Salad

This nutritious salad is easily portable. Take it to work as a lunch or turn it into a light dinner served with grilled meats. The fresh parsley and coriander add a delicate touch.

Preparation: 10 to 15 minutes
Cooking Time: 5 minutes
Makes: 8 1-cup (250-mL) servings

1	pkg (350 g) frozen corn niblets	1
1	can (19 oz/540 mL) kidney beans, drained and rinsed	1
1	can (19 oz/540 mL) black beans, drained and rinsed	1
1	large tomato, diced	1
3	green onions, finely chopped	3
1	jalapeño pepper, finely chopped	1
3 tbsp	finely chopped fresh parsley	45 mL
1 tbsp	finely chopped fresh coriander	15 mL
2 tbsp	Becel oil	30 mL
2 tbsp	red wine vinegar	30 mL
2 tbsp	fresh lime juice	30 mL
1 tsp	grated lime rind	5 mL
1	clove garlic, minced	1
1/2 tsp	freshly ground black pepper	2 mL
	Salt to taste	

Nutrients per serving
Calories 176
Protein 8.6 g
Fat 3.8 g
  PUFA 1.7 g
  MUFA 1.5 g
  SFA 0.4 g
Carbohydrates 29.4 g
Fibre 7.3 g
Cholesterol 0 mg
Sodium 230 mg
Potassium 398 mg
Excellent source of folacin. Contains a very high amount of dietary fibre.

Cook the corn according to package directions and drain. In a large bowl, mix corn, kidney beans, black beans, tomato, green onions, jalapeño, parsley and coriander.

In a small bowl, whisk together oil, vinegar, lime juice and rind, garlic and pepper. Pour over bean mixture; toss gently to coat vegetables. Refrigerate for at least 1 hour. Season with salt to taste before serving.

SUBSTITUTION: Replace kidney beans or black beans with chick-peas, lima beans or white kidney beans.

SERVING SUGGESTION: For a main meal, add 1 can (170 g) water-packed tuna, drained, or 1/4 lb (125 g) thinly sliced grilled chicken.

Tabbouleh

This crunchy Middle Eastern salad is made from bulgur (cracked toasted wheat). It has the wonderful taste and aroma of fresh herbs. Serve with barbecued chicken or lamb or for lunch with grilled eggplant.

³/₄ cup	bulgur	175 mL
1¹/₂ cups	boiling water	375 mL
1 cup	diced seedless cucumber (unpeeled)	250 mL
³/₄ cup	chopped seeded tomatoes	175 mL
¹/₂ cup	diced sweet yellow pepper	125 mL
2	green onions, chopped	2
¹/₂ cup	finely chopped fresh parsley	125 mL
2 tbsp	finely chopped fresh mint	30 mL
3 tbsp	Becel oil	45 mL
2 tbsp	lemon juice	30 mL
1	clove garlic, mashed	1
	Salt and freshly ground black pepper to taste	
	Mint sprigs for garnish	

Preparation: 55 minutes
Refrigeration Time: 2 hours
Serves: 8

Place bulgur in a large bowl; stir in boiling water. Cover and let stand for 30 minutes. Drain well through strainer; use a spoon to press out excess water. Cool to room temperature.

Stir in cucumber, tomatoes, yellow pepper, green onions, parsley and mint.

In a small bowl, combine oil, lemon juice and garlic; pour over salad and mix well. Season with salt and pepper. Refrigerate 2 hours or up to 1 day. Remove from refrigerator 15 minutes before serving. Garnish with mint sprigs.

VARIATION: Add ³/₄ cup (175 mL) chick-peas or 2 tbsp (30 mL) toasted pine nuts.

Nutrients per serving
Calories 97
Protein 2.1 g
Fat 5.1 g
 PUFA 2.3 g
 MUFA 2.2 g
 SFA 0.5 g
Carbohydrates 12.1 g
Fibre 2.2 g
Cholesterol 0 mg
Sodium 7 mg
Potassium 140 mg
Good source of vitamin C and folacin.

> **Bulgur** is made of whole wheat berries that have been steamed and hulled, then dried and cracked. As bulgur contains wheat germ, it can turn rancid. Buy bulgur that smells fresh and nutty. Store in an airtight container in refrigerator or freezer.

Crunchy Vegetable Summer Salad

This salad may be prepared a day ahead and left in the refrigerator. Serve it in a glass bowl to show off all the layers of colourful vegetables.

Preparation: about 30 minutes
Cooking Time: 5 minutes
Makes 12 1/2-cup (125-mL) servings

1	large tomato, sliced	1
1	small sweet onion, finely chopped	1
1	medium fennel bulb, thinly sliced	1
1	medium carrot, thinly sliced	1
1/4 lb	mushrooms, thinly sliced	125 g
1/2	seedless cucumber, thinly sliced	1/2
1	medium sweet red pepper, cut in thin strips	1
1	pkg (350 g) frozen corn niblets	1
DRESSING		
1/2 cup	frozen orange juice concentrate, thawed	125 mL
2 tbsp	Becel oil	30 mL
2 tbsp	fresh lemon juice	30 mL
1 tbsp	honey mustard	15 mL
1 tbsp	anchovy paste	15 mL
2 tsp	dried basil (or 2 tbsp/30 mL chopped fresh)	10 mL
1 tsp	celery seeds	5 mL
1/2 tsp	hot pepper flakes	2 mL
	Salt and pepper to taste	

Nutrients per serving
Calories 97
Protein 2.7 g
Fat 2.7 g
  PUFA 1.1 g
  MUFA 1.1 g
  SFA 0.2 g
Carbohydrates 17.6 g
Fibre 2.6 g
Cholesterol 1 mg
Sodium 54 mg
Potassium 383 mg
Excellent source of vitamin A and vitamin C.

In a large glass bowl place a layer of tomatoes. Sprinkle with onion. Arrange layers of fennel, carrot, mushrooms, cucumber and red peppers on top of cucumber.

Cook corn according to package directions. Drain and spoon over the salad.

In a small bowl, whisk together dressing ingredients; pour over vegetables. Chill for at least 3 hours or overnight. Season with salt and pepper. Serve at room temperature.

VARIATION: One or 2 finely chopped jalapeño peppers may be added with the onions.

Coleslaw with Apples and Dried Cranberries

The piquant taste of the dried cranberries adds flavour and freshness to this old-time favourite. Double the recipe for large gatherings.

4 cups	finely shredded green cabbage	1 L
2 tbsp	finely chopped red onion	30 mL
1	stalk celery, thinly sliced	1
1/3 cup	dried cranberries	75 mL
1	red apple, chopped	1

DRESSING

1/4 cup	apple cider vinegar	50 mL
1 tbsp	Dijon mustard	15 mL
2 tsp	granulated sugar	10 mL
1/4 tsp	*each:* salt, pepper	1 mL
3 tbsp	Becel oil	45 mL

Preparation: 15 minutes
Serves: 6

In a large bowl, combine cabbage, onion, celery, dried cranberries and apple.

In a small bowl, whisk together dressing ingredients until sugar dissolves.

Pour dressing over salad and toss well. Cover and chill.

TIME SAVER TIP: Use a food processor to shred the cabbage, or use packaged sliced cabbage from the produce section of your grocery store.

SERVING SUGGESTION: Serve coleslaw over grilled sausage on a bun or with turkey, chicken or pork burgers.

Nutrients per serving
Calories 113
Protein 0.9 g
Fat 6.8 g
    PUFA 3.1 g
    MUFA 3.0 g
    SFA 0.6 g
Carbohydrates 13.4 g
Fibre 1.9 g
Cholesterol 0 mg
Sodium 142 mg
Potassium 187 mg
Good source of vitamin C.

Roasted Potato Salad

Here is a very flavourful way to prepare potato salad without mayonnaise. There is no need to peel the potatoes, so the preparation time is cut down considerably.

Preparation: 10 minutes
Cooking Time: 40 minutes
Serves: 6

1¹/₂ lb	baking potatoes (russet, Yukon Gold, Idaho), skins on, cut into wedges (about 1"/2.5 cm thick)	750 g
¹/₂ tsp	salt	2 mL
4 tsp	Becel oil, divided	20 mL
¹/₂	red onion, thinly sliced	1/2
¹/₂ cup	chopped fresh basil or chopped fresh parsley	125 mL
1 tbsp	red wine vinegar	15 mL
1 tbsp	Dijon mustard	15 mL
2 to 3	cloves garlic, minced	2 to 3
¹/₄ tsp	*each:* salt, freshly ground black pepper	2 mL

Nutrients per serving
Calories 127
Protein 2.4 g
Fat 3.3 g
  PUFA 1.6 g
  MUFA 1.4 g
  SFA 0.3 g
Carbohydrates 22.6 g
Fibre 2.4 g
Cholesterol 0 mg
Sodium 328 mg
Potassium 393 mg
Good source of vitamin B6.

Preheat oven to 400°F (200°C). Spread potatoes evenly on a baking sheet. Season with salt and toss with 2 tsp (10 mL) of the oil. Bake for 35 to 40 minutes or until potatoes are tender, stirring occasionally to promote even browning and prevent sticking. Remove from oven and place potatoes in a medium serving bowl. Add onion and basil or parsley.

In a small bowl, whisk together remaining 2 tsp (10 mL) oil, vinegar, mustard and garlic. Pour over potato mixture and toss well. Season with salt and pepper. Serve warm or at room temperature. Refrigerate unused portions up to 2 days.

Wild Rice Salad

The earthy flavour of the wild rice, the crunchiness of the vegetables and almonds along with the sweetness of the raisins make this salad an intriguing flavour experience. A bonus is that it travels well, so it's great for picnics and brown-bagging it.

1 cup	wild rice	250 mL
2¹/₂ cups	water	625 mL
¹/₂ cup	finely chopped red onion	125 mL
1	stalk celery, diced	1
2	carrots, diced	2
1	sweet red pepper, diced	1
¹/₂ cup	raisins	125 mL
1 tbsp	Becel oil	15 mL
3 tbsp	balsamic vinegar	45 mL
3	cloves garlic, minced	3
¹/₃ cup	toasted slivered almonds	75 mL
	Salt and freshly ground black pepper to taste	

Preparation: 25 minutes
Cooking Time: 45 to 60 minutes
Chilling Time: 2 hours
Serves: 8

In a medium saucepan, combine rice and water. Bring to a boil, stir once, reduce heat to low and simmer, covered, for 45 to 60 minutes or until rice is tender and puffed and most of the liquid has been absorbed. Drain any extra liquid. Let stand, covered, for 5 minutes. Fluff with a fork.

In a large non-metallic bowl, place cooked rice with remaining ingredients and toss well. Refrigerate at least 2 hours to allow flavours to blend.

TIME SAVER TIP: Use parboiled wild rice.

Nutrients per serving
Calories 173
Protein 4.8 g
Fat 4.8 g
  PUFA 1.6 g
  MUFA 2.6 g
  SFA 0.5 g
Carbohydrates 30.1 g
Fibre 2.7 g
Cholesterol 0 mg
Sodium 16 mg
Potassium 314 mg
Excellent source of vitamin A and vitamin C.

> **Toasted Almonds:** Place almonds on a baking sheet and bake in a preheated 400°F (200°C) oven for 5 to 7 minutes or until golden brown, shaking pan occasionally.

Warm Asian Steak Salad

A nice summer salad, great for lunch or a light supper. Serve the salad immediately after tossing.

Preparation: 20 minutes
Cooking Time: 38 minutes
Serves: 4

DRESSING

1/2 cup	orange juice	125 mL
1/2 tbsp	*each:* minced fresh ginger (or 1/2 tsp/2 mL ground ginger), rice wine vinegar	7 mL
2	cloves garlic, minced	2
2 tsp	*each:* light soy sauce, sesame oil, liquid honey	10 mL
1 tsp	Becel oil	5 mL
Dash	hot pepper sauce (optional)	Dash

STEAK

3/4 lb	sirloin tip steak, trimmed of all visible fat	375 g

SALAD

12 cups	mixed greens (romaine, arugula, red leaf, frisée, etc)	3 L
1/2 lb	asparagus, trimmed, cooked and cut in 1-inch (2.5-cm) pieces	250 g
1	sweet red pepper, cut in strips	1
1/2	seedless cucumber, thinly sliced	1/2
3	green onions, thinly sliced	3
1/4 cup	chopped fresh coriander (optional)	50 mL
1 tbsp	toasted sesame seeds for garnish	15 mL

Whisk together all dressing ingredients. Pour 1/4 cup (50 mL) of dressing over steak in a shallow non-metallic dish, turning to coat. Cover and marinate in refrigerator for 2 hours or overnight. Reserve remaining dressing.

Grill steak 3 to 4 minutes per side for medium (if steak is about 1 inch/2.5 cm thick). Let steak rest for a few minutes before carving. Slice thinly on the diagonal.

Nutrients per serving
Calories 208
Protein 22.1 g
Fat 6.8 g
 PUFA 1.6 g
 MUFA 2.5 g
 SFA 1.6 g
Carbohydrates 16.6 g
Fibre 4.1 g
Cholesterol 40 mg
Sodium 156 mg
Potassium 1005 mg
Excellent source of vitamin A, vitamin C, niacin, vitamin B6, folacin, vitamin B12, magnesium, iron and zinc. Contains a high amount of dietary fibre.

In a serving dish, toss reserved dressing with salad greens, asparagus, red pepper, cucumber, green onions and coriander (if using). Arrange steak over salad, garnish with toasted sesame seeds and serve immediately.

TIME SAVER TIP: Purchase ready-to-use mesclun mix in the produce section of most supermarkets.

Toasted Sesame Seeds: Place sesame seeds in a small nonstick skillet over medium-high heat and cook for 4 to 5 minutes, watching closely and shaking pan occasionally, until seeds are golden brown.

Couscous and Chick-pea Salad

When combined with colourful and crunchy vegetables, light and fluffy couscous makes an interesting salad. This one is particularly good with grilled meats or poultry.

Preparation: 25 minutes
Serves: 6

1 tbsp	Becel margarine	15 mL
3	cloves garlic, minced	3
1 1/4 cups	water	300 mL
1 cup	couscous	250 mL
1/2 tsp	salt	2 mL
1 cup	chopped fresh coriander or parsley	250 mL
1/4 cup	chopped fresh mint	50 mL
4	green onions, chopped	4
1	medium tomato, seeded and chopped	1
1/2	seedless cucumber, diced	1/2
1	can (19 oz/540 mL) chick-peas, drained and rinsed	1
2 tbsp	lemon juice	25 mL
1 tbsp	Becel oil	15 mL
2 tsp	ground cumin	10 mL
1/2 cup	crumbled lower-fat feta cheese (17.5% MF)	125 mL
	Salt and freshly ground black pepper to taste	

Nutrients per serving
Calories 289
Protein 11.4 g
Fat 8.9 g
  PUFA 2.5 g
  MUFA 3.0 g
  SFA 2.8 g
Carbohydrates 41.5 g
Fibre 4.3 g
Cholesterol 9 mg
Sodium 421 mg
Potassium 299 mg
Excellent source of folacin.
  Contains high amount of
  dietary fibre.

In a medium saucepan, melt margarine over medium heat. Sauté garlic for 1 minute. Add water and bring to a boil. Stir in couscous and salt. Remove from heat, cover and let stand for 5 minutes. Fluff with a fork.

Transfer couscous to a large bowl and toss with remaining ingredients. (Salad may be stored in refrigerator for up to 1 day.)

> **Couscous** is semolina flour that has been mixed with salt water and then tossed and rubbed into tiny pellets. You can find instant couscous in most major grocery stores. Couscous is extremely quick to prepare (see page 95) and can be served in many different ways.

Meatless Mains—
Pasta, Grains, Beans

Fast

When You Have More Time

Squash Lasagna with Leeks and Spinach

Vegetarian lasagna with the goodness of butternut squash and spinach flavoured with sage. Well worth the effort!

Preparation: 40 minutes
Cooking Time: 40 minutes
Serves: 8

VEGETABLE FILLING

1	medium butternut squash	1
2 tsp	Becel margarine, regular or salt-free	10 mL
1	bunch leeks (white and light green part), sliced	1
2	cloves garlic, minced	2
1/2 cup	dry white wine or chicken broth	125 mL
1 tbsp	dried sage (or 3 tbsp/45 mL chopped fresh)	15 mL
1	pkg (300 g) frozen chopped spinach, thawed and well drained	1
	Salt and freshly ground black pepper to taste	

Nutrients per serving
Calories 334
Protein 19.3 g
Fat 9.1 g
  PUFA 1.5 g
  MUFA 2.8 g
  SFA 4.2 g
Carbohydrates 45.1 g
Fibre 4.9 g
Cholesterol 20 mg
Sodium 453 mg
Potassium 612 mg
Excellent source of vitamin A, folacin, calcium and magnesium. Contains a high amount of dietary fibre.

SAUCE

1 tbsp	Becel margarine, regular or salt-free	15 mL
1/4 cup	all-purpose flour	50 mL
3 cups	1% milk	750 mL
3/4 cup	grated 40%-less-fat Parmesan cheese, divided	175 mL
1/4 tsp	*each:* salt, freshly ground black pepper	1 mL
Pinch	ground nutmeg	Pinch
9	lasagna noodles, cooked	9
1 1/2 cups	shredded partly skimmed mozzarella cheese	375 mL

Peel and seed squash and cut into 1/2-inch (2-cm) cubes. You should have 5 cups (1.25 L).

For Vegetable Filling, in a large skillet, melt margarine over medium heat. Sauté leeks and garlic 4 minutes. Add squash, wine or broth and sage; cover and simmer 15 minutes, stirring occasionally, or until squash is tender. Stir in spinach. Season with salt and pepper.

For Sauce, melt margarine in a medium saucepan. Whisk together flour and milk; add to saucepan. Cook, stirring, until mixture comes to a boil and is thickened. Remove from heat and whisk in ½ cup (125 mL) of the Parmesan cheese, salt, pepper and nutmeg.

Preheat oven to 375°F (190°C). In greased 13- x 9-inch (3.5-L) baking pan, spread ½ cup (125 mL) of the sauce. Top with 3 lasagna noodles, half of the vegetable mixture, half the mozzarella cheese and ½ cup (125 mL) of the sauce. Repeat layers, ending with noodles. Spread remaining sauce over top, making sure to cover noodles.

Cover and bake 30 minutes. Uncover; sprinkle with remaining Parmesan cheese and bake 10 minutes longer or until bubbling.

TIME SAVER TIP: A great time-saver is the shredded cheese available in the dairy section of the supermarket. Oven-ready (no-boil) lasagna noodles may also be used to save cooking time.

KITCHEN TIP: To make cutting squash easier, place squash in microwave oven on High for 3 minutes to soften. Or purchase already peeled pieces of squash, often available in the produce section of your supermarket.

Pasta with Spinach, Tomatoes and Feta

A fusion of Greek and Italian ingredients! If you don't have spinach, use chopped broccoli instead. Just cook, covered, until broccoli is tender.

Preparation: 20 minutes
Cooking Time: 15 to 20 minutes
Serves: 4

¾ lb	penne or fusilli	375 g
1 tsp	Becel oil	5 mL
3	cloves garlic, minced	3
3	large tomatoes, diced	3
1	pkg (10 oz/284 g) fresh spinach, trimmed, washed and coarsely chopped	1
¼ cup	fresh basil, chopped (or 1 tbsp/15 mL dried)	50 mL
½ cup	crumbled lower-fat feta cheese (17.5% MF)	125 mL
¼ tsp	salt	1 mL
	Freshly ground black pepper to taste	

Nutrients per serving
Calories 402
Protein 15.8 g
Fat 5.7 g
  PUFA 1.4 g
  MUFA 1.5 g
  SFA 2.0 g
Carbohydrates 72.9 g
Fibre 7.3 g
Cholesterol 7 mg
Sodium 475 mg
Potassium 690 mg
Excellent source of vitamin A, thiamine, folacin, magnesium and iron. Contains a very high amount of dietary fibre.

Cook pasta in lightly salted boiling water until tender but still firm to the bite, about 7 minutes. Drain.

Meanwhile, in a large deep saucepan or Dutch oven, heat oil over low heat. Sauté the garlic for 2 minutes or until softened and fragrant (do not allow garlic to brown). Stir in tomatoes, spinach, and dried basil (if using), and cook, stirring, 3 minutes more or until spinach starts to wilt. Stir in fresh basil (if using) and feta. Toss well with drained pasta. Season with salt and pepper. Serve immediately.

Fusilli with Tomatoes and Basil

Try this scrumptious pasta recipe instead of tomato pasta sauce.

2 tbsp	Becel oil, divided	30 mL
1	medium onion, finely chopped	1
2	cloves garlic, minced	2
6	small plum tomatoes, diced	6
1	sweet green pepper, diced	1
1	pkg (10 oz/284 g) fresh spinach, cleaned, trimmed and chopped	1
1/2 tsp	freshly ground black pepper	2 mL
1/2 tsp	ground nutmeg	2 mL
1 lb	fusilli or rotini	500 g
3/4 cup	basil, thinly shredded	175 mL
2 tbsp	balsamic vinegar	30 mL
2 tbsp	lemon juice	30 mL
1/2 cup	grated Parmesan cheese	125 mL

Preparation: 25 to 30 minutes
Cooking Time: 15 to 20 minutes
Serves: 6

In a large nonstick skillet over medium heat, heat 1 tbsp (15 mL) of the oil. Add onion and sauté 5 minutes or until softened. Add garlic and sauté 1 minute more. Add tomatoes and green pepper; cook, stirring occasionally, 10 minutes or until vegetables begin to soften. Stir in spinach, black pepper and nutmeg. Cook just until the spinach begins to wilt.

Meanwhile, cook the pasta in lightly salted boiling water until tender but firm, about 7 minutes. Drain well.

In a large bowl, toss pasta with the hot tomato mixture, basil, vinegar, remaining 1 tbsp (15 mL) of the oil and lemon juice. Add the Parmesan cheese; toss well. Serve immediately.

Nutrients per serving
Calories 401
Protein 15.4 g
Fat 8.6 g
  PUFA 2.7 g
  MUFA 2.9 g
  SFA 2.3 g
Carbohydrates 66.1 g
Fibre 5.9 g
Cholesterol 7 mg
Sodium 390 mg
Potassium 487 mg
Excellent source of vitamin A, thiamine, folacin, magnesium and iron. Contains a high amount of dietary fibre.

Super-Simple Tomato Sauce

Versatility is the key to this sauce—change it to suit your mood. If you like a little heat, add the hot pepper flakes. Try adding peppers or mushrooms while cooking the other vegetables. Or add a can of chunk tuna or cooked extra-lean ground beef. The sauce freezes very well, so keep some stashed in the freezer for emergencies.

Preparation: 10 minutes
Cooking Time: 30 minutes
Makes: 3$^{1}/_{2}$ cups (875 mL)

2 tsp	Becel margarine or oil	10 mL
1	small onion, diced	1
2	cloves garlic, minced	2
1	small carrot, diced	1
$^{1}/_{2}$	stalk celery, diced	$^{1}/_{2}$
$^{1}/_{2}$ cup	dry white or red wine (optional)	125 mL
1	can (28 oz/796 mL) diced plum tomatoes	1
$^{3}/_{4}$ tsp	Italian seasoning	4 mL
$^{1}/_{4}$ tsp	hot pepper flakes (optional)	1 mL

Nutrients per serving
(1 cup/250 mL)
Calories 83
Protein 2.7 g
Fat 2.7 g
  PUFA 1.1 g
  MUFA 0.9 g
  SFA 0.4 g
Carbohydrates 14.2 g
Fibre 3.2 g
Cholesterol 0 mg
Sodium 407 mg
Potassium 596 mg
Excellent source of
  vitamin A.

In a medium saucepan, heat margarine over medium heat. Add onion, garlic, carrot and celery. Cook, stirring occasionally, for 5 minutes or until vegetables are beginning to soften.

Increase heat to high. Add wine (if using), stirring occasionally. Cook until wine has nearly evaporated. Add tomatoes and their juice and Italian seasoning. For a spicier sauce, add hot pepper flakes. Bring to a boil, reduce heat and simmer, uncovered and stirring occasionally, until sauce has thickened slightly, about 20 minutes. Serve over pasta.

Vegetable Cheese Pie

This delicious vegetable pie will fill your kitchen with a wonderful aroma while it's baking. The eggplant slices form the "crust," and the filling of tomatoes, onions, fennel, basil and cheese combine to deliver a tasty pie.

1	medium eggplant (about 1 lb/500 g)	1
1 tbsp	Becel margarine, melted	15 mL
1	small fennel bulb (or ½ large bulb), chopped	1
½ cup	finely chopped red onion	125 mL
¼ cup	finely shredded fresh basil	50 mL
1 tbsp	lemon juice	15 mL
3	medium plum tomatoes, sliced	3
1 cup	shredded partly skimmed mozzarella cheese (about ¼ lb/125 g)	250 mL

Topping

¼ cup	fresh white breadcrumbs	50 mL
2 tbsp	grated Parmesan cheese	30 mL
1 tsp	dried oregano (or 1 tbsp/15 mL chopped fresh)	5 mL
½ tsp	freshly ground black pepper	2 mL

Preparation: 20 to 25 minutes
Cooking Time: 30 to 35 minutes
Serves: 6 to 8

Preheat oven to 450°F (220°C). Cut eggplant crosswise into ¼-inch (5-mm) slices. Toss eggplant slices with melted margarine; place on a baking sheet. Bake for 10 minutes. Place fennel and onion on baking sheet; bake 5 to 7 minutes more or until fennel is softened. Remove from oven. Reduce temperature to 375°F (190°C).

In a 9-inch (23-cm) pie plate arrange eggplant slices, slightly overlapping, to cover bottom and sides. Mix fennel and onion with the basil and lemon juice; spoon over eggplant slices. Arrange the tomato slices over the fennel mixture. Sprinkle mozzarella cheese over tomato slices.

To make the Topping: In a small bowl, mix together breadcrumbs, Parmesan cheese, oregano and pepper. Sprinkle over mozzarella. Bake for 30 to 35 minutes or until topping is lightly browned. Let rest 10 minutes before slicing.

Nutrients per serving
Calories 138
Protein 8.9 g
Fat 6.8 g
   PUFA 1.0 g
   MUFA 2.1 g
   SFA 3.3 g
Carbohydrates 11.5 g
Fibre 3.4 g
Cholesterol 14 mg
Sodium 208 mg
Potassium 422 mg
Good source of calcium.

Roasted Vegetable Crustless Quiche

Without the pastry, this version of the traditional Quiche Lorraine is much lower in fat. Serve with whole grain rolls and a salad for balanced meal.

Preparation: 25 minutes
Cooking Time: 35 minutes
Serves: 6

VEGETABLES

1	medium onion, thinly sliced	1
2 cups	broccoli florets	500 mL
1	sweet red pepper, diced	1

CUSTARD

4	eggs	4
2	egg whites	2
3/4 cup	skim milk	175 mL
3/4 cup	evaporated skim milk	175 mL
1/4 tsp	*each:* salt, freshly ground black pepper, ground nutmeg	1 mL
1 tbsp	Dijon mustard	15 mL

FILLING

1/2 cup	shredded Gruyère cheese	125 mL
1/4 cup	diced smoked lower-fat ham (optional)	50 mL
1/4 cup	chopped green onion	50 mL
1 tbsp	grated Parmesan cheese	15 mL
1 tsp	Becel margarine, melted	5 mL

Nutrients per serving
Calories 167
Protein 14.1 g
Fat 8 g
 PUFA 1.1 g
 MUFA 2.8 g
 SFA 3.3 g
Carbohydrates 9.7 g
Fibre 1.0 g
Cholesterol 159 mg
Sodium 384 mg
Potassium 358 mg
Excellent source of vitamin C, riboflavin, vitamin B12 and calcium.

Preheat oven to 400°F (200°C). Spread onion, broccoli and red pepper on 15- x 10-inch (38- x 25-cm) baking sheet lined with parchment paper. Roast for 15 minutes, turning once. Remove from oven; do not turn off oven.

Meanwhile, make Custard: In a medium bowl, whisk together eggs, egg whites, skim milk, evaporated skim milk, salt, pepper, nutmeg and mustard.

Using a pastry brush, grease a 10-inch (25-cm) quiche dish with margarine. Arrange roasted vegetables in quiche dish. Top with Gruyère, ham (if using) and green onions. Carefully pour in custard mixture. Sprinkle with Parmesan cheese. Bake for 30 to 35 minutes or until knife inserted near centre comes out clean. Serve immediately.

KITCHEN TIP: **Before serving, drain any excess liquid that results from the higher water content of the egg whites.**

Sunday Brunch Menu

Brunch is a wonderful and casual way to entertain family and friends. Try this nutritional menu for a late morning get-together that requires little fuss.

Zesty Bean Dip (page 40) with **Tortilla Crisps** (page 41) and raw
   vegetables
Roasted Vegetable Crustless Quiche (page 86)
Tabbouleh (page 71)
Cranberry Orange Muffins (page 158)
Fresh fruit

Mediterranean Vegetable Wraps

Wonderful Mediterranean vegetables are quickly cooked, then rolled up in tortillas with feta cheese and topped with pesto.

Preparation: 20 minutes
Cooking Time: 25 minutes
Makes 6 wraps

2 tsp	Becel oil	10 mL
1	medium onion, chopped	1
1/2 cup	*each:* chopped sweet red and green pepper	125 mL
1 1/2 cups	chopped peeled eggplant	375 mL
1 cup	chopped zucchini	250 mL
2	cloves garlic, minced	2
1 tsp	dried basil (or 1 tbsp/15 mL chopped fresh)	5 mL
1/2 tsp	*each:* dried thyme, dried oregano	2 mL
1	medium tomato, chopped	1
1/4 tsp	*each:* salt, freshly ground black pepper	1 mL
6	low-fat flour tortillas (6-inch/15-cm)	6
6 tbsp	crumbled feta cheese	90 mL
2 tbsp	prepared low-fat pesto	30 mL

Nutrients per (1 wrap)
serving
Calories 180
Protein 5.2 g
Fat 7.4 g
  PUFA 1.8 g
  MUFA 3.0 g
  SFA 2.2 g
Carbohydrates 24.1 g
Fibre 2.7 g
Cholesterol 8 mg
Sodium 381 mg
Potassium 254 mg
Good source of vitamin C
  and thiamine.

Preheat oven to 400°F (200°C).

In a large nonstick skillet, heat oil over medium-high heat. Sauté onion and peppers 3 minutes. Add eggplant, zucchini, garlic, basil, thyme and oregano; sauté 5 minutes more. Add tomato, salt and pepper. Simmer 5 minutes or until thickened and vegetables are tender. Cool slightly.

Spoon filling onto centre of tortillas, dividing evenly. Sprinkle each with about 1 tbsp (15 mL) of the feta. Wrap up, secure with wooden picks, and place on a baking sheet. Bake for 10 minutes or until crisp and heated through. To serve, cut each wrap in half and top with 1 tsp (5 mL) pesto.

Low-Fat Pesto: To prepare a small quantity of low-fat pesto for this recipe, combine in a small food processor until well blended: 2 tbsp (30 mL) each Becel oil and chopped fresh basil, 1 tbsp (15 mL) 40%-less-fat grated Parmesan cheese, 2 tsp (10 mL) pine nuts and 1 clove garlic, minced.

Stuffed Sweet Peppers

These tasty peppers are stuffed with a high-fibre mixture of brown rice, lentils and corn. Prepared salsa and canned legumes (peas, beans and lentils) provide extra convenience. Make these as hot or as mild as you like.

4	large sweet green peppers	4
1 tbsp	Becel margarine	15 mL
1/2 cup	diced onion	125 mL
1	clove garlic, minced	1
2 cups	cooked brown parboiled rice	500 mL
1 1/2 cups	coarsely shredded Monterey Jack cheese	375 mL
1 cup	mild salsa (or to taste)	250 mL
3/4 cup	cooked lentils	175 mL
1/2 cup	frozen corn kernels	125 mL
1/4 cup	chopped fresh parsley	50 mL
	Salt and freshly ground black pepper to taste	

Preparation: 30 to 35 minutes (includes cooking of rice)
Oven Cooking Time: 25 to 30 minutes
Serves: 4

Preheat oven to 400°F (200°C).

Cut tops from peppers; remove seeds and membranes. Trim bottoms so peppers stand straight. Boil peppers in large pot of boiling water for 2 minutes; drain, cut side down, on paper towel.

In a large nonstick skillet over medium heat, melt margarine. Add onions and sauté 5 minutes. Add garlic and sauté 1 minute more.

In a large bowl, combine onion mixture, rice, 1 cup (250 mL) of the Monterey Jack cheese, salsa, lentils, corn, parsley, salt and pepper. Fill prepared peppers with rice mixture. Place in 8-inch (20-cm) square baking dish; add a little water to pan. Cover with foil and bake for 25 minutes. Top each pepper with 2 tbsp (30 mL) of the remaining cheese. Bake, uncovered, for 5 minutes. Serve immediately.

SUBSTITUTIONS
- For extra spice, use hot salsa or add minced jalapeño peppers to the rice mixture.
- Substitute black beans for the lentils.
- Substitute Cheddar or mozzarella cheese for the Monterey Jack.
- Substitute fresh coriander for the parsley.

Nutrients per serving
Calories 412
Protein 19.1 g
Fat 17.1 g
  PUFA 2.1 g
  MUFA 5.2 g
  SFA 8.7 g
Carbohydrates 48.8 g
Fibre 7.3 g
Cholesterol 38 mg
Sodium 425 mg
Potassium 662 mg
Excellent source of vitamin A, vitamin C, niacin, vitamin B6, folacin, calcium, magnesium, iron and zinc. Contains a very high amount of dietary fibre.

Two-Bean Chili

Meat lovers won't miss the meat in this spicy chili. Serve with small bowls of thinly sliced green onion, chopped coriander, shredded light Cheddar and light sour cream to use as toppings. This chili freezes beautifully.

Preparation: 15 minutes
Cooking Time: 45 minutes
Serves: 8

1 tbsp	Becel oil or margarine	15 mL
1	medium onion, diced	1
2	sweet peppers, preferably 1 red and 1 green, diced	2
3	cloves garlic, minced	3
2	jalapeño peppers, seeded and minced	2
2	cans (each 28 oz/796 mL) plum tomatoes	2
1	can (19 oz/540 mL) black beans, rinsed and drained	1
1	can (19 oz/540 mL) kidney beans, rinsed and drained	1
2 tbsp	chili powder	30 mL
1 tbsp	ground cumin	15 mL
2 tsp	dried oregano (or 2 tbsp/30 mL chopped fresh)	10 mL
1/2 cup	bulgur	125 mL
4	green onions, thinly sliced	4
1/2 cup	finely chopped fresh coriander	125 mL
	Salt to taste	

Nutrients per serving
Calories 228
Protein 12.0 g
Fat 3.3 g
 PUFA 1.2 g
 MUFA 0.9 g
 SFA 0.3 g
Carbohydrates 41.6 g
Fibre 11.3 g
Cholesterol 0 mg
Sodium 616 mg
Potassium 906 mg
Excellent source of vitamin A, vitamin C, folacin, magnesium and iron. Contains a very high amount of dietary fibre.

In a large saucepan, heat margarine over medium heat. Add onion, sweet peppers, garlic and jalapeño; cook, stirring occasionally, 5 minutes or until tender. Add tomatoes and their juice, crushing tomatoes with the back of a spoon. Add black beans, kidney beans, chili powder, cumin and oregano. Bring to a boil. Cover, reduce heat and simmer, stirring occasionally, for 20 minutes.

Stir in bulgur and continue to cook, uncovered and stirring occasionally, until bulgur is tender, about 20 minutes.

Stir in green onions and coriander. Add salt to taste. Serve immediately.

Meat and Poultry

Fast

When You Have More Time

Mango Chicken

Mangoes add a delectable touch to this chicken dish. Chicken breasts are coated in a wonderful spice blend, then quickly sautéed with mango and coriander. In the summer, use fresh peaches (instead of mango) and basil for a change.

Preparation: 10 minutes
Cooking Time: 10–15
   minutes
Serves: 4

1/2 tsp	ground cumin	2 mL
1/2 tsp	ground ginger	2 mL
1/4 tsp	dried thyme (or 3/4 tsp/3 mL chopped fresh)	1 mL
Pinch	*each:* ground nutmeg, cayenne pepper	Pinch
4	boneless, skinless chicken breasts (about 1 lb/500 g)	4
2 tsp	Becel margarine	10 mL
1	ripe but firm mango, peeled and cut into chunks	1
2	green onions, thinly sliced	2
	Salt to taste	
1/4 cup	chopped fresh coriander	50 mL
	Squeeze of lime	

Nutrients per serving
Calories 204
Protein 30.9 g
Fat 4.2 g
  PUFA 1.3 g
  MUFA 1.3 g
  SFA 0.9 g
Carbohydrates 9.7 g
Fibre 1.3 g
Cholesterol 77 mg
Sodium 94 mg
Potassium 499 mg
Excellent source of niacin
  and vitamin B6.

In a small dish, stir together spices. Sprinkle both sides of chicken breasts with spice mixture. Heat margarine in a large nonstick skillet over medium-high heat. Add chicken breasts and cook, turning occasionally, until both sides are a deep golden brown and chicken is no longer pink inside, about 10 to 15 minutes.

Add mango and green onions. Cook, stirring, just until heated through, about 1 minute. Remove from heat. Sprinkle with salt, coriander and a squeeze of lime. Serve immediately.

Oven-baked Orange Ginger Chicken Thighs

For an easy midweek supper, serve these Asian-style chicken thighs over rice along with a quick vegetable stir-fry. If you wish, use bone-in skinless chicken breasts instead of thighs and bake for 35 to 40 minutes.

2 tsp	finely grated orange rind	10 mL
1/4 cup	freshly squeezed orange juice	50 mL
2 tbsp	hoisin sauce	30 mL
1 tbsp	lime or lemon juice	15 mL
1 tbsp	finely minced fresh ginger	15 mL
2	cloves garlic, minced	2
8	skinless chicken thighs, bone-in	8
	Chopped fresh chives or parsley for garnish	

Preparation: 12 minutes
Cooking Time: 2 minutes
Baking Time: 30 minutes
Serves: 4

Preheat oven to 350°F (180°C).

In a small bowl, whisk together orange rind, orange juice, hoisin sauce, lime juice, ginger and garlic. Pour into a baking dish just large enough to hold the chicken. Add chicken and turn to coat.

Bake, uncovered, turning occasionally, 30 minutes or until chicken is no longer pink inside. Pour liquid into a small saucepan; boil until thickened slightly, about 1 minute. Serve chicken with sauce spooned over top. Garnish with chopped chives or parsley.

Nutrients per serving
Calories 176
Protein 22.4 g
Fat 6.2 g
 PUFA 1.6 g
 MUFA 1.9 g
 SFA 1.5 g
Carbohydrates 6.4 g
Fibre .5 g
Cholesterol 95 mg
Sodium 229 mg
Potassium 323 mg
Excellent source of niacin.
 Good source of vitamin
 B6, vitamin B12,
 pantothenic acid and
 zinc.

Moroccan Chicken and Vegetable Skillet

This quick-cooking chicken stew uses the wonderfully fragrant spices of Morocco. Serve over couscous for an authentic meal.

Preparation: 15 minutes
Cooking Time: 10 minutes
Serves: 4

1 tsp	fennel seeds (optional)	5 mL
1 tsp	ground cumin	5 mL
1/4 tsp	*each:* ground cinnamon, cayenne pepper	1 mL
2 tsp	Becel oil	10 mL
2	boneless, skinless chicken breasts (12 oz/375 g), cut in 1-inch (2.5-cm) cubes	2
1	medium onion, chopped	1
2	cloves garlic, minced	2
3/4 cup	sodium-reduced chicken broth	175 mL
1	medium zucchini, sliced	1
2–3	medium carrots, julienned	2–3
1/4 cup	raisins	50 mL
1/4 tsp	salt	1 mL
2 tsp	cornstarch	10 mL
	Chopped fresh coriander for garnish	

Nutrients per serving
Calories 202
Protein 22 g
Fat 4.2 g
   PUFA 1.4 g
   MUFA 1.5 g
   SFA 0.7 g
Carbohydrates 19.4 g
Fibre 2.8 g
Cholesterol 49 mg
Sodium 372 mg
Potassium 631 mg
Excellent source of
   vitamin A, niacin and
   vitamin B6.

Place the fennel seeds (if using) on a cutting board and break them by cutting once or twice with a large, heavy knife. Or if you have a mortar and pestle, give them a couple of grinds to lightly crush and release the aroma.

In a small bowl, mix crushed fennel seeds, cumin, cinnamon and cayenne. Set aside.

In a large nonstick skillet, heat oil over medium-high heat. Brown chicken with onion and garlic about 5 minutes. Stir in fennel mixture and sauté 1 minute. Add broth, zucchini, carrots, raisins and salt; bring to a boil. Cover and simmer over low heat, stirring once, 5 minutes or until vegetables are tender.

Dissolve cornstarch in 1 tbsp (15 mL) water; stir cornstarch mixture into pan and cook until thickened.

Serve over prepared couscous or rice and garnish with chopped coriander.

TIME SAVER TIP: Use packaged baby peeled carrots.

KITCHEN TIP: To prepare the couscous bring 1 cup (250 mL) water to a boil. Stir in ¾ cup (175 mL) couscous. Cover, remove from heat and let stand 5 minutes. Fluff with a fork.

Chicken with Zesty Tomato Sauce

A super summertime recipe, when tomatoes are ripe and full of flavour and basil is growing in the garden. For a change of pace try this versatile sauce with your favourite pasta and sprinkle with finely chopped fresh herbs, or replace the chicken with your favourite white fish and reduce the cooking time by half.

Preparation: 15 to 20 minutes
Cooking Time: 45 minutes
Serves: 2

5	medium tomatoes	5
1 tbsp	Becel margarine	15 mL
4	boneless, skinless chicken thighs	4
¼ lb	white and brown mushrooms, thinly sliced	125 g
1 tbsp	balsamic vinegar	15 mL
6	large fresh basil leaves, thinly shredded (or 1 tsp/5 mL dried)	6
2 tbsp	coarsely chopped fresh parsley	30 mL
1 tsp	light brown sugar	5 mL
2 to 3	drops hot pepper sauce	2 to 3
	Salt and freshly ground black pepper to taste	

Nutrients per serving
Calories 275
Protein 25.2 g
Fat 12.1 g
  PUFA 4 g
  MUFA 4.1 g
  SFA 2.4 g
Carbohydrates 18.2 g
Fibre 4.5 g
Cholesterol 95 mg
Sodium 172 mg
Potassium 1002 mg
Excellent source of vitamin A, vitamin C, riboflavin, niacin, vitamin B6, pantothenic acid, magnesium, iron and zinc. Contains a very high amount of dietary fibre.

Dice 1 tomato and set aside. Dice remaining tomatoes and place in a large nonstick skillet. Cook over medium-low heat, uncovered, for 15 minutes or until mixture is reduced by half. Press tomatoes through a sieve to remove seeds and skin. (Final puréed mixture should measure approximately 1 cup/250 mL.)

In same skillet on medium-high heat, melt margarine. Sauté chicken and mushrooms until chicken is lightly browned. Add tomato purée, reserved diced tomato, vinegar, basil, parsley, sugar, hot pepper sauce, salt and pepper. Bring mixture to a boil; reduce heat to medium-low, cover and continue to cook, stirring occasionally, for 20 to 25 minutes or until chicken is cooked and tender. Serve with couscous or brown rice.

Opposite: Super Simple Tomato Sauce (page 84)
Overleaf: Mango Chicken (page 92)

urried Chicken and Vegetable Couscous

A light and quick dinner, perfect for busy weeknights. Vary the vegetables in this simple yet hearty main dish according to whatever you have at home. It's particularly good with green beans, cubed acorn or butternut squash or cauliflower.

2	small boneless, skinless chicken breasts, cut into strips	2
2 tsp	curry powder	10 mL
1 tsp	ground cumin	5 mL
1 tbsp	Becel oil	15 mL
1	small onion, finely chopped	1
2 cups	sodium-reduced chicken broth	500 mL
3 cups	chopped broccoli	750 mL
1	sweet red pepper, chopped	1
¼ cup	golden raisins	50 mL
1 tbsp	Becel light margarine	15 mL
1 cup	couscous	250 mL
	Salt and freshly ground black pepper to taste	

Preparation: 20 minutes
Cooking Time: 15 minutes
Serves: 4

In a small bowl, toss chicken with half of the curry and half of the cumin.

In a large nonstick skillet, heat oil on medium-high heat. Brown chicken until no longer pink; remove and set aside.

Add onion to skillet and sauté over low heat for 3 minutes. Add chicken broth, broccoli, red pepper, raisins, margarine, cooked chicken, couscous and remaining curry and cumin. Bring to a boil, cover and simmer for 3 minutes. Remove from heat and let stand, covered, 5 minutes. Season to taste with salt and pepper. Fluff with a fork before serving.

Nutrients per serving
Calories 348
Protein 22.1 g
Fat 6.4 g
  PUFA 2.4 g
  MUFA 2.2 g
  SFA 0.7 g
Carbohydrates 51.2 g
Fibre 4.4 g
Cholesterol 34 mg
Sodium 407 mg
Potassium 572 mg
Excellent source of vitamin C, niacin, vitamin B6 and folacin. Contains a high amount of dietary fibre.

Opposite: Moroccan Chicken and Vegetable Skillet (page 94)
Overleaf: Pad Thai (Asian Noodles) (page 98)

Pad Thai (Asian Noodles)

It's the exotic ingredients that makes this trendy dish so popular.

Preparation: 20 minutes
Cooking Time: about 15 minutes
Serves: 4

2 tbsp	*each:* soy sauce, lemon juice	30 mL
1 tbsp	*each:* ketchup, packed light brown sugar	15 mL
2 tsp	dark sesame oil	10 mL
1/4 tsp	hot pepper flakes	1 mL
5 oz	wide rice stick noodles	150 g
1 tbsp	Becel oil	15 mL
1	boneless, skinless chicken breast, thinly sliced	1
6 oz	extra-firm tofu, cut into 1/2-inch (1-cm) cubes	175 g
2	cloves garlic, minced	2
1 tbsp	minced fresh ginger	15 mL
1/2	*each:* sweet red and yellow peppers, thinly sliced	1/2
12	cooked jumbo shrimp, shells and tails removed (optional)	12
1 cup	bean sprouts	250 mL
1/4 cup	*each:* chopped roasted peanuts, sliced green onion, chopped fresh coriander	50 mL

Nutrients per serving
Calories 346
Protein 16.9 g
Fat 13 g
PUFA 5.3 g
MUFA 5.2 g
SFA 1.7 g
Carbohydrates 42.2 g
Fibre 3.2 g
Cholesterol 19 mg
Sodium 710 mg
Potassium 400 mg
Excellent source of vitamin C, niacin, vitamin B6 and magnesium.

In a small bowl, mix together soy sauce, lemon juice, ketchup, brown sugar, sesame oil and hot pepper flakes; set aside.

Cook rice noodles in boiling salted water for 2 to 3 minutes or until tender. Drain noodles, cover and set aside.

In a large nonstick skillet or wok over medium heat, heat oil. Cook chicken just until it changes colour; remove with slotted spoon.

Add tofu, garlic and ginger to pan; sauté 1 minute. Stir in peppers; sauté 2 minutes. Stir in shrimp (if using), sprouts and cooked rice noodles. Pour in reserved soy sauce mixture. Toss well and heat through. Serve immediately, sprinkled with peanuts, green onion and coriander.

- Purchase rice stick noodles at Asian markets and some supermarkets.
- If available, use Asian chili paste in place of hot pepper flakes and garlic.

SUBSTITUTION: For a meatless version, omit the chicken and replace with 2 eggs. Beat the eggs and cook in the centre of the wok after the red peppers are cooked, stirring to scramble; stir into mixture. If you don't like tofu, just skip it.

Tofu, also know as soy bean curd, is made by adding a coagulant to fresh soy milk. Tofu, a very versatile food, is rich in high-quality protein and is a good source of B vitamins and iron. Tofu is also low in saturated fat and contains no cholesterol.

There are 2 common types of tofu: regular (firm or extra firm) and silken (soft). Silken tofu has a smoother, custard-like texture. Choose firm or extra firm tofu when you'd like it to hold its shape, for example if you are grilling or stir-frying. Use silken tofu for dips, shakes, spreads, sauces, desserts or whenever you'd prefer a creamier consistency.

Tofu is available in the produce section of most grocery stores.

Chicken Fajitas

Fajitas are a fun dinner idea for casual get-togethers. Let everyone assemble their own. Keep in mind it's best to choose lower-fat garnishes like salsa, chopped tomatoes and coriander rather than high-fat ones like sour cream and shredded cheese.

Preparation: 15 minutes
Cooking Time: 15 to 20 minutes
Serves: 4

2 tbsp	Becel oil, divided	30 mL
1	large onion, thinly sliced	1
1	medium sweet green pepper, cut into thin strips	1
1	medium sweet red pepper, cut into thin strips	1
1	medium clove garlic, minced	1
8	whole wheat tortillas (6-inch/15-cm)	8
3	medium boneless, skinless chicken breasts, cut into thin strips	3
1 tbsp	lime juice	15 mL
2 tsp	chili powder	10 mL
1/2 tsp	ground cumin	2 mL
1/4 tsp	cayenne pepper	1 mL

TOPPINGS: **Chopped tomatoes, salsa, low-fat yogurt, light sour cream (use sparingly), shredded low-fat Cheddar cheese (use sparingly), chopped fresh coriander.**

Nutrients per serving
Calories 427
Protein 32.5 g
Fat 13.2 g
 PUFA 5.2 g
 MUFA 5.2 g
 SFA 1.8 g
Carbohydrates 43.5 g
Fibre 3.7 g
Cholesterol 66 mg
Sodium 379 mg
Potassium 593 mg
cellent source of vitamin
 thiamine, niacin,
 amin B6.

Preheat oven to 250°F (120°C).

In a large skillet, over medium-high heat, heat 1 tbsp (15 mL) of the oil. Add onion, peppers, and garlic; cook, stirring, for 3 to 5 minutes or until tender. Remove from pan.

Wrap tortillas in foil. Bake for 10 minutes or until heated through.

Add remaining 1 tbsp (15 mL) of the oil to skillet. Add chicken and cook 2 minutes or until browned. Stir in lime juice, chili powder, cumin and cayenne. Return vegetables to pan and heat through.

To serve, spoon one-quarter of chicken mixture onto centre of each warm tortilla. Add desired toppings and fold tortillas over filling.

ork and Sweet Potatoes Latin American Style

This flavourful stew of pork and sweet potatoes also has coriander and black beans to give an authentic Latin American flair. It bakes in the oven for easy fix-and-forget preparation.

2 tsp	Becel oil	10 mL
1 lb	lean pork loin (trimmed of all visible fat), cut into 1-inch (2.5-cm) cubes	500 g
1	medium onion, sliced	1
2	cloves garlic, minced	2
1	can (19 oz/540 mL) diced tomatoes	1
1 tsp	*each:* chili powder, ground cumin	5 mL
1/4 tsp	cayenne	1 mL
2	medium sweet potatoes (1 lb/500 g), peeled and cut in 1-inch (2.5-cm) cubes	2
1	can (19 oz/540 mL) black beans, drained and rinsed	1
1/3 cup	fresh coriander, chopped	75 mL

Preparation: 20 minutes
Cooking Time: 1 hour 10 minutes
Serves: 4

Preheat oven to 350°F (180°C).

In a large nonstick skillet, heat oil over medium-high heat. Brown pork with onion and garlic 5 minutes. Stir in tomatoes, chili powder, cumin and cayenne; bring to a boil. Stir in sweet potatoes. Pour mixture into 3-quart (3-L) casserole.

Bake covered, stirring once, for 45 minutes. Stir in black beans and coriander. Bake, covered, 10 to 15 minutes longer or until pork and potatoes are tender and beans are hot. Serve immediately.

SERVING SUGGESTION: **Serve with a tossed green salad and toasted pita wedges for a complete meal.**

Nutrients per serving
Calories 456
Protein 36.6 g
Fat 10.1 g
  PUFA 2.2 g
  MUFA 4.1 g
  SFA 2.7 g
Carbohydrates 55.6 g
Fibre 10.2 g
Cholesterol 66 mg
Sodium 534 mg
Potassium 1379 mg
Excellent source of vitamin A, vitamin C, thiamine, riboflavin, niacin, vitamin B6, folacin, vitamin B12, magnesiu iron and zinc. Contai very high amount of dietary fibre.

Meat and Poultry

Turkey Burgers with Cranberry Dijon Topping

These burgers are moist and especially delicious topped with this cranberry-flavoured mustard topping. The cranberries add a refreshing piquant flavour to the wilder flavour of the turkey. Don't press down on the burger while it fries, because you will squeeze out all the juices.

Preparation: 20 minutes (including topping)
Cooking Time: 8 to 10 minutes
Serves: 4

CRANBERRY DIJON TOPPING

1 cup	fresh or frozen cranberries	250 mL
1/3 cup	granulated sugar	75 mL
1/3 cup	water	75 mL
3 tbsp	Dijon mustard	45 mL

TURKEY BURGERS

2 tsp	Becel oil	10 mL
3/4 cup	diced onion	175 mL
1	clove garlic, minced	1
1 1/2 lb	ground turkey	750 g
1	egg, beaten	1
1/4 cup	dry breadcrumbs or quick-cooking oatmeal	50 mL
1/4 cup	finely chopped fresh parsley	50 mL
	Salt and freshly ground black pepper to taste	

Nutrients per serving
Calories 573
Protein 39.3 g
Fat 20.5 g
  PUFA 5.6 g
  MUFA 7.8 g
  SFA 4.8 g
Carbohydrates 55.7 g
Fibre 2.5 g
Cholesterol 167 mg
Sodium 649 mg
Potassium 486 mg
 cellent source of niacin,
 itamin B6, folacin,
 amin B12, iron and

To prepare Cranberry Dijon Topping: In a small saucepan, combine cranberries, sugar and water. Bring to a boil, reduce heat and simmer 10 minutes. Transfer to a bowl and let cool. In food processor, coarsely purée cranberry mixture with mustard. Refrigerate until ready to use. (May be made ahead and refrigerated for up to 2 weeks. Makes 1 cup/500 mL.)

In a large nonstick skillet over medium heat, heat oil. Add onions and sauté for 5 minutes or until softened. Stir in garlic; sauté 1 minute.

In a large bowl, combine turkey, egg, breadcrumbs, parsley and onion mixture. Mix well; season with salt and pepper. Shape into 4 patties.

In the same skillet or on lightly oiled grill pan, cook patties over medium heat for 4 to 5 minutes per side. Serve on burger buns or kaisers spread with Becel margarine. Top patties with Cranberry Dijon Topping and lettuce or alfalfa sprouts.

SERVING SUGGESTION: **Shape mixture into meatballs and fry on all sides in a large, deep non-stick skillet with 2 tsp/10mL Becel oil. Brown meatballs in two batches if necessary. Use Cranberry Dijon Topping as a dipping sauce.**

KITCHEN TIP: **Uncooked patties may be frozen for up to 3 months. Wrap in freezer wrap.**

Casual Summer Barbecue

Entertaining during the summer can easily take on a last minute, spontaneous edge once you include your backyard barbecue. Try this fast and easy light-hearted summer menu with family and friends.

Roasted Garlic and Herb Dip with assorted raw vegetables (page 35)
Turkey Burgers with Cranberry Dijon Topping (page 102)
Potato, Green Bean and Red Onion Salad (page 69)
Seasonal Fruit Crisp (page 145)

Pork Scallopini with Wild Mushrooms

Quickly cooked thinly sliced pork is topped with wild mushrooms and a savoury sauce. When purchasing scallopini, choose ones that are no thicker than $1/4$ inch (5 mm). Serve with rice or medium egg noodles.

Preparation: 15 minutes
Cooking Time: 10 minutes
Serves: 2 to 3

1/2 cup	chicken broth	125 mL
1 tbsp	grainy Dijon mustard	15 mL
1 tbsp	tomato paste	15 mL
2 tsp	Worcestershire sauce	10 mL
1 1/2 tsp	cornstarch	7 mL
1 tbsp	Becel margarine, divided	15 mL
1/2 lb	mushrooms (such as oyster, portobello or button), sliced	250 g
1/2 lb	thin pork scallopini	250 g
	Paprika	
	Salt and freshly ground black pepper to taste	
2 tbsp	light sour cream (5% MF)	30 mL
	Chopped chives or parsley for garnish	

Nutrients per serving
Calories 258
Protein 29.3 g
Fat 11.1 g
  PUFA 3.2 g
  MUFA 4.4 g
  SFA 2.7 g
Carbohydrates 9.9 g
Fibre 2.1 g
Cholesterol 93 mg
Sodium 480 mg
Potassium 890 mg
Excellent source of
  thiamine, riboflavin,
  niacin, vitamin B5,
  vitamin B12,
  pantothenic acid, iron
  and zinc.

Whisk together chicken broth, mustard, tomato paste, Worcestershire sauce and cornstarch; set aside. In a large nonstick skillet, melt half the margarine over medium-high heat. Add mushrooms; cook, stirring frequently, until mushrooms are tender and golden brown, 6 to 8 minutes. Set aside in a bowl.

Lightly season both sides of pork with paprika, salt and pepper. Melt remaining margarine in skillet over medium-high heat. Add pork and cook, 2 to 3 minutes each side, until just a hint of pink remains inside. Remove from pan and set aside with mushrooms.

Stir broth mixture then add to pan, stirring until mixture boils and thickens slightly, 30 to 60 seconds. Remove from heat and stir in sour cream. Return mushrooms and pork to skillet, turning to coat with sauce. Gently heat through if necessary. Serve immediately, sprinkled with chives.

BBQ Pork with Fresh Mango Salsa

A delicious way to prepare pork on the barbecue or under the broiler. The piquant taste of mango adds flavour and vitality to this California cuisine–inspired dish.

MARINADE

¼ cup	sodium-reduced soy sauce	50 mL
1 tbsp	lime juice	15 mL
1 tbsp	minced fresh ginger	15 mL
1	clove garlic, minced	1
1 tsp	honey	5 mL
½ tsp	freshly ground black pepper	2 mL
¾ lb	boneless pork loin centre cut chops, 1½ inches (3 cm) thick, trimmed of all visible fat	375 g

SALSA

1	ripe but firm mango, peeled and diced	1
¼ cup	diced sweet red pepper	50 mL
2	green onions, thinly sliced	2
2 tbsp	chopped fresh coriander or basil	30 mL
1 tbsp	lime juice	15 mL

Preparation: 20 minutes
Marinating Time: 1 hour
Cooking Time: 10 minutes
Serves: 4

Combine all Marinade ingredients. Toss pork in marinade and chill, covered, for at least 1 hour or overnight.

Combine Salsa ingredients and set aside.

Drain pork and discard marinade. Barbecue pork over medium heat, or broil 3 inches (8 cm) from broiler, for 5 minutes on each side or until juices run clear. Cut pork in thin slices and serve with Fresh Mango Salsa and Tropical Rice (page 138).

SUBSTITUTION: **Instead of mango, use diced fresh papaya.**

Nutrients per serving
Calories 164
Protein 19.2 g
Fat 5.1 g
  PUFA 0.6 g
  MUFA 2.3 g
  SFA 1.7 g
Carbohydrates 10.5 g
Fibre 1.3 g
Cholesterol 49 mg
Sodium 113 mg
Potassium 492 mg
Excellent source of
  thiamine and niacin.

Beef Tenderloin in Orange Sauce

This spicy-sweet beef recipe is incredibly easy to prepare.

Preparation: 15 minutes
Cooking Time: 10 to 15
   minutes
Marinating Time: 5
   minutes
Serves: 2

SAUCE

½ cup	orange juice	125 mL
1 tbsp	lime juice	15 mL
1 tbsp	grated orange rind	15 mL
1 tsp	grated lime rind	5 mL
1 tbsp	light soy sauce	15 mL
1 tbsp	light or orange marmalade spread	15 mL
1 tbsp	grated fresh or prepared horseradish	15 mL
½ tsp	dried sage leaves	2 mL
½ tsp	hot pepper flakes	2 mL
1 cup	sodium-reduced beef broth	250 mL

BEEF

½ lb	beef tenderloin, cut into strips	250 g
6 oz	broad egg noodles	175 g
1 tbsp	Becel margarine	15 mL

Nutrients per serving
Calories 593
Protein 37 g
Fat 17.3 g
  PUFA 3.7 g
  MUFA 6.4 g
  SFA 4.5 g
Carbohydrates 70.8 g
Fibre 5.6 g
Cholesterol 137 mg
Sodium 1060 mg
Potassium 777 mg
Excellent source of
  thiamine, riboflavin,
  niacin, vitamin B5,
  folacin, vitamin B12,
  magnesium, iron and
  zinc. Contains a high
  amount of dietary fibre.

In a large bowl, mix together Sauce ingredients. Add beef and stir gently to coat. Let beef marinate in sauce for 5 minutes. Remove beef and drain well. Pour sauce through a sieve into a small saucepan. Bring to a boil; boil until reduced to ½ cup (125 mL), 12 to 15 minutes.

Meanwhile, bring pot of lightly salted water to a boil. Add noodles and cook until tender but firm, about 7 minutes. Drain well.

In a nonstick skillet over medium heat, melt margarine. Add beef and sauté, stirring frequently, until beef is lightly browned on all sides. Stir in reduced sauce. Spoon meat mixture over noodles and serve.

KITCHEN TIPS

- To preserve fresh horseradish: Peel and grate a horseradish root. Mix with ¹/₂ tsp (2 mL) salt and ¹/₄ tsp (1 mL) granulated sugar. Put into glass or ceramic container with screw-top lid. Cover with white vinegar. Cover surface with a piece of parchment paper. Replace lid. Store in the refrigerator until required. Will keep for several months.

- Look for prepared horseradish in the refrigerated section of your grocery store. Do not use the creamed type.

SERVING SUGGESTION: Serve beef with steamed broccoli, green beans or Oriental mixed vegetables (to save time, use the frozen variety).

Asian Inspired Menu

The unique flavours of Asian cuisine will make this menu a popular one for family and friends. Leftovers of the Beef Tenderloin in Orange Sauce are particularly good cold and used for sandwiches or a picnic.

Hot and Sour Chicken Soup (page 62)
Beef Tenderloin in Orange Sauce (page 106) served with broad noodles or rice
Spicy Sesame Green Beans (page 128) or
Ginger Carrots with Broccoli and Sesame Seeds (page 132)
Mandarin oranges

Veal Osso Bucco

Osso bucco is Italian for "bone with hole"—the marrow found inside the bone is considered a delicacy. Serve with mashed potatoes or rice.

Preparation: 30 minutes
Cooking Time: 1½ hours
Serves: 6

3 tbsp	Becel oil, divided	45 mL
2 cups	diced carrots (4 to 5 medium)	500 mL
1½ cups	diced onion	375 mL
2	stalks celery, diced	2
3	large cloves garlic, minced	3
1 tbsp	dried thyme (or 3 tbsp/45 mL chopped fresh)	15 mL
3	bay leaves	3
6	veal shank (osso bucco) (about 3 lb/1.5 kg)	6
	Salt and freshly ground black pepper	
¼ cup	all-purpose flour	50 mL
1 cup	dry white wine	250 mL
1 cup	(approx.) sodium-reduced beef broth	250 mL
1	can (28 oz/796 mL) diced tomatoes	1

GREMOLATA

½ cup	chopped fresh parsley	125 mL
1 tbsp	grated lemon rind	15 mL
2	cloves garlic, minced	2
	Fresh thyme sprigs for garnish	

Nutrients per serving
Calories 390
Protein 38.2 g
Fat 16.9 g
  PUFA 3.9 g
  MUFA 6.8 g
  SFA 4.7 g
Carbohydrates 19.3 g
Fibre 3.7 g
Cholesterol 147 mg
Sodium 532 mg
Potassium 1152 mg
Excellent source of vitamin A, riboflavin, niacin, vitamin B6, folacin, vitamin B12, magnesium, iron and zinc.

Preheat oven to 375°F (190°C).

In a large oven-proof casserole over medium heat, heat 1 tbsp (15 mL) of the oil. Add carrots, onion and celery; sauté until carrots are almost soft, about 7 minutes. Add garlic, thyme and bay leaves; sauté 2 minutes more.

In a large skillet over medium-high heat, heat remaining 2 tbsp (30 mL) of the oil. Season veal with salt and pepper. Coat with flour, shaking off excess. Cook veal about 4 minutes on each side or until browned. Transfer to casserole.

Add wine and beef broth to skillet and bring to a boil, stirring to loosen any brown bits; pour over veal. Add tomatoes to casserole. If necessary, add more broth to almost cover veal.

Cover and bake for $1^1/_2$ hours or until meat is very tender and starting to separate from bones. Before serving, remove bay leaves. If necessary, boil sauce on stovetop to reduce slightly.

To make Gremolata, combine parsley, lemon rind and garlic in bowl.

To serve, arrange veal on a platter. Spoon sauce and gremolata on top. Garnish with fresh thyme sprigs.

Comforting Italian Winter Menu

Canadians' love for the rich flavours of Italian cuisine is still going strong. It's no wonder when there is such a vast selection of simple, hearty dishes to bring to the table. Delight your dinner companions with this exquisitely delicious meal.

Roasted Red Pepper Crostini (page 34)
Veal Osso Bucco (page 108)
Herbed Onion Potatoes (page 136)
Mixed green salad with light balsamic vinaigrette
Poached Pears with Caramel Sauce (page 150)

Mustard-marinated Steak

This steak is delicious on the barbecue, served with fresh corn on the cob and sliced tomatoes. Barbecue over medium heat for 4 to 5 minutes per side for rare.

Preparation: 5 minutes
Marinating Time: 4 hours
Cooking Time: 13 to 17 minutes
Serves: 4

1/4 cup	Becel oil	50 mL
2 tbsp	red wine vinegar	30 mL
2 tbsp	Dijon mustard	30 mL
2 tsp	Worcestershire sauce	10 mL
1/2 tsp	dried thyme (or 1 1/2 tsp/7 mL chopped fresh)	2 mL
3/4 lb	boneless sirloin steak or flank steak	375 g

Nutrients per serving
Calories 162
Protein 16 g
Fat 10 g
  PUFA 3.2 g
  MUFA 4.5 g
  SFA 2. g
Carbohydrates 0.5 g
Fibre 0 g
Cholesterol 39 mg
Sodium 93 mg
Potassium 218 mg
Excellent source of vitamin B12 and zinc.

In a small bowl, whisk together oil, vinegar, mustard, Worcestershire sauce and thyme.

Trim as much fat as possible from steak. Place in shallow glass dish just large enough to hold steak. Pour marinade over meat, turning to coat. Cover and refrigerate at least 4 hours or preferably overnight, turning occasionally.

Drain meat. Place meat on broiler pan. Broil 3 inches (8 cm) from heat for 13 to 17 minutes for medium doneness, turning once. To serve, slice beef thinly across the grain.

Steak Grilling Tips
- grill or broil steaks over a preheated medium-high heat. Turn once or twice using tongs rather than a fork (piercing meat will allow juices to escape).
- when grilling plain (not marinated) steak, season with pepper and other seasonings *before* grilling.
- to grill or broil steaks: a 1–inch (2.5 cm) thick steak, 7 to 9 minutes per side for medium (internal temperature 160 F°/70°C); 9 to 11 minutes per side for well done (internal temperature of 170° F/75°C).
- do not grill marinated meat past medium because the meat will become dry.

Fish and Seafood

Fast

Curried Crab Cakes with Chutney Sauce

Enjoy a little taste of the South with these wonderful and easy-to-prepare crab cakes. The chutney sauce adds just the right tanginess. Use your favourite chutney, and chop pieces that are too large.

Preparation: 15 minutes
Cooking Time: 8 minutes
Serves: 4

CHUTNEY SAUCE

2 tbsp	*each:* fat-free plain yogurt, fat-free mayonnaise	30 mL
1 tbsp	mango chutney	15 mL
2 tsp	balsamic vinegar	10 mL

CRAB CAKES

1/2 lb	fresh or frozen crab meat, drained and flaked	250 g
1	egg white, lightly beaten	1
1/2 cup	fine dry breadcrumbs	125 mL
2	green onions, chopped	2
2 tbsp	lime juice	30 mL
1 tsp	curry powder	5 mL
1/4 tsp	*each:* salt, cayenne	1 mL
2 tsp	Becel margarine, regular or salt free	10 mL

Nutrients per serving
Calories 186
Protein 17.4 g
Fat 5.1 g
  PUFA 1.6 g
  MUFA 1.8 g
  SFA 0.9 g
Carbohydrates 17.2 g
Fibre 0.6 g
Cholesterol 94 mg
Sodium 747 mg
Potassium 224 mg
Excellent source of niacin, vitamin B12 and zinc.

In a small bowl, combine Chutney Sauce ingredients, mixing well; set aside.

For crab cakes, combine crab meat, egg white, breadcrumbs, green onions, lime juice, curry powder, salt and cayenne; mix well. Form into 4 patties or 8 smaller patties.

In a nonstick skillet, melt margarine over medium-high heat. Brown crab cakes, about 4 minutes per side. Serve warm with chutney sauce.

SUBSTITUTION: Use 2 cans (120 g each) crab meat, drained and flaked.

SERVING SUGGESTIONS: Serve with rice flavoured with a little lime rind and a salad. (Sauce recipe can also be used as an accompaniment for grilled fish.)

Pasta with Scallops and Snow Peas

This simple pasta sauce is made with scallops and snow peas, flavoured with the delicate taste of ginger and basil.

1¹/₂ cups	small pasta shells	375 mL	
2 cups	snow peas (about ¹/₂ lb/250 g), trimmed and cut in half diagonally	500 mL	
2 tsp	Becel margarine, regular or salt free	10 mL	
1	medium onion, chopped	1	
2 tsp	minced fresh ginger	10 mL	
³/₄ lb	bay scallops	375 g	
3 tbsp	dry white wine or water	45 mL	
1 tbsp	all-purpose flour	15 mL	
³/₄ cup	2% milk	175 mL	
¹/₄ tsp	salt	1 mL	
Pinch	freshly ground black pepper	Pinch	
¹/₄ cup	coarsely chopped fresh basil (or 1¹/₂ tsp/ 7 mL dried)	50 mL	

Preparation: 10 minutes
Cooking Time: 15 minutes
Serves: 4

Cook pasta in a pot of lightly salted boiling water, stirring occasionally, until firm to the bite, 5 to 8 minutes. Add snow peas in the last 2 minutes of cooking time. Drain.

Meanwhile, in a large skillet, melt margarine over medium heat. Sauté onion 4 minutes. Add ginger and sauté 1 minute more. Add scallops and white wine; bring to a boil and simmer 3 minutes or until scallops are almost cooked.

Dissolve flour in milk; add to skillet with salt and pepper. Cook, stirring, until thickened slightly and bubbling. Stir in cooked pasta, snow peas and basil; heat through. Serve immediately.

SUBSTITUTIONS
- Use other small pasta shapes such as macaroni or penne.
- Instead of scallops, smoked salmon bits work well in this sauce.

Nutrients per serving
Calories 301
Protein 22.9 g
Fat 4.2 g
  PUFA 1.4 g
  MUFA 1.1 g
  SFA 1.0 g
Carbohydrates 40.4 g
Fibre 3.7 g
Cholesterol 31 mg
Sodium 324 mg
Potassium 577 mg
Excellent source of niacin, folacin, vitamin B12 and magnesium.

Scallops with White Wine and Tarragon Sauce

Enjoy tender scallops in a creamy herb and wine sauce—without the cream!
Serve with rice or pasta.

Preparation: 20 minutes
Cooking Time: about 20 minutes
Serves: 4

1 lb	large sea scallops (about 16)	500 g
2 tbsp	Becel margarine, divided	30 mL
1/2 cup	diced shallots	125 mL
1/2 cup	diced carrots	125 mL
2 tbsp	minced sweet red pepper	30 mL
1	small clove garlic, minced	1
2 tbsp	all-purpose flour	30 mL
1/2 cup	dry white wine	125 mL
1 cup	2% milk	250 mL
2 tbsp	chopped fresh parsley	30 mL
1 tbsp	chopped fresh tarragon (or 1 tsp dried)	15 mL
	Salt and freshly ground black pepper to taste	
2 tbsp	snipped fresh chives for garnish	30 mL

Nutrients per serving
Calories 230
Protein 22.2 g
Fat 7.6 g
  PUFA 2.6 g
  MUFA 2.6 g
  SFA 1.6 g
Carbohydrates 13.8 g
Fibre 1.3 g
Cholesterol 42 mg
Sodium 276 mg
Potassium 606 mg
Excellent source of vitamin A, vitamin B12 and magnesium.

Rinse scallops with cold water; dry with paper towel. In a large skillet over medium heat, melt 1 tbsp (15 mL) of the margarine. Cook scallops 1 minute on each side. Remove and set aside.

Melt remaining 1 tbsp (15 mL) margarine in skillet. Add shallots, carrots and red pepper; sauté 5 minutes. Stir in garlic; sauté 1 minute. Stir in flour; cook 1 minute. Pour in wine, stirring constantly. Gradually stir in milk, stirring constantly, until sauce comes to a boil. Reduce heat and simmer, stirring occasionally, for 3 minutes.

Stir in scallops, parsley and tarragon; cook 30 seconds. Season to taste with salt and pepper. Pour into serving dish or spoon onto plates and garnish with chopped chives. Serve immediately.

SUBSTITUTION: Replace tarragon with fresh dill.

Fettuccine with Mussels

Serve this in large shallow bowls with crusty bread to sop up the wonderful broth, and pair with a green salad for an elegant but simple dinner. Place a bowl in the centre of the table for the empty shells.

¾ lb	fettuccine	375 g
1 tbsp	Becel margarine	15 mL
4	cloves garlic, minced	4
¾ cup	dry white wine	175 mL
1	can (28 oz/796 mL) tomatoes, chopped, with juices	1
¼ tsp	hot pepper flakes	1 mL
2 lb	mussels, scrubbed and beards removed	1 kg
½ cup	*each:* coarsely chopped fresh parsley and basil	125 mL
	Salt and freshly ground black pepper to taste	

Preparation: 15 minutes
Cooking Time: 15 minutes
Serves: 4

Cook fettuccine in plenty of lightly salted boiling water, stirring occasionally, until tender but firm to the bite, 5 to 8 minutes. Drain.

Meanwhile, in a large saucepan or Dutch oven over medium-low heat, melt margarine. Sauté garlic for 2 minutes. Stir in wine, tomatoes and pepper flakes; bring to a boil. Stir in mussels, cover and cook on medium-high heat, shaking pan occasionally, until mussels open, about 3 to 5 minutes. (Discard any mussels that do not open.) Remove from heat and stir in parsley and basil. Season to taste with salt and pepper.

Divide pasta evenly into 4 bowls. Pour mussels and sauce over fettuccine and serve immediately.

SERVING SUGGESTION: If you like, prepare the mussels and sauce only and serve as an appetizer for 4.

SAFETY TIP: Mussels are purchased alive and must stay that way until they are cooked. When cleaning mussels, discard any that do not close tightly when tapped and any with broken shells. Discard any mussels that do not open when cooked, as they are not safe to eat.

Nutrients per serving
Calories 462
Protein 20.9 g
Fat 6.3 g
  PUFA 2.4 g
  MUFA 1.7 g
  SFA 1.0 g
Carbohydrates 76.6 g
Fibre 6.3 g
Cholesterol 18 mg
Sodium 770 mg
Potassium 838 mg
Excellent source of vitamin C, thiamine, niacin, folacin, vitamin B12, magnesium, iron and zinc. Contains a very high amount of dietary fibre.

Salmon with Spiced Fresh Pineapple

Want to try something completely different? The simple yet sharp flavour of pineapple complements the richness of salmon in this dish—and makes an arresting flavour combination.

Preparation: about 15 minutes
Cooking Time: 15 to 20 minutes
Serves: 2

3/4 cup	short-grain rice or basmati rice	175 mL
2 cups	water	500 mL
1/4 tsp	salt	1 mL
1 1/4 cups	chopped fresh pineapple, divided	300 mL
1 tbsp	Becel margarine	15 mL
2 tbsp	light soy sauce	30 mL
1 tbsp	packed light brown sugar	15 mL
1 tbsp	minced fresh ginger (or 1 tsp/5 mL ground ginger)	15 mL
1/4 tsp	*each:* ground cinnamon, allspice	1 mL
2	salmon fillets (4 oz/125 g each)	2
2 tbsp	finely chopped fresh coriander	30 mL
2 tbsp	finely chopped fresh mint	30 mL
	Salt and freshly ground black pepper to taste	
	Sprigs fresh mint for garnish	

Nutrients per serving
Calories 558
Protein 28.7 g
Fat 13.5 g
  PUFA 5.4 g
  MUFA 4.8 g
  SFA 2 g
Carbohydrates 78.7 g
Fibre 2.6 g
Cholesterol 62 mg
Sodium 968 mg
Potassium 823 mg
Excellent source of thiamine, riboflavin, niacin, vitamin B6, vitamin B12, pantothenic acid and magnesium.

Bring the rice, water and salt to a boil in a saucepan. Reduce heat to a simmer, cover and cook rice, stirring occasionally, for 15 to 20 minutes or until rice is cooked.

Meanwhile, set aside 1/4 cup (50 mL) of the pineapple. In a nonstick skillet, melt margarine over medium heat. Add remaining pineapple, soy

> **Coriander, cilantro or Chinese parsley:** Three names for the same herb. It is closely related to caraway, fennel, dill and anise. The leaves resemble those of flat-leaf parsley.

sauce, brown sugar, ginger, cinnamon and allspice. Cook, stirring, for 3 minutes. Add the salmon and cook for 4 to 5 minutes on each side or until fish flakes easily with a fork.

Stir the reserved pineapple, coriander and mint into the cooked rice. Season rice and fish with salt and pepper and serve garnished with fresh mint springs.

SUBSTITUTION: If you wish, use canned diced pineapple, drained, instead of chopped fresh pineapple.

Lime and Ginger Grilled Salmon

Sometimes the simplest ingredients complement fresh fish the best. Do not marinate fish for longer than 30 minutes or it may start to go mushy.

Preparation: 10 minutes
Marinating Time: 15 minutes
Grilling Time: 8 minutes
Serves: 2

1 tsp	finely grated lime rind	5 mL
¼ cup	lime juice (about 1 large lime)	50 mL
2 tsp	Becel oil	10 mL
1 tsp	minced fresh ginger	5 mL
1	jalapeño pepper, seeded and finely minced	1
2	salmon steaks (6 oz/175 g each)	2

Nutrients per serving
Calories 338
Protein 30.8 g
Fat 21.4 g
  PUFA 8.1 g
  MUFA 8.1 g
  SFA 3.8 g
Carbohydrates 4.4 g
Fibre 0.4 g
Cholesterol 87 mg
Sodium 86 mg
Potassium 81 mg
Excellent source of thiamine, niacin, vitamin B6, vitamin B12 and pantothenic acid.

Whisk together lime rind, lime juice, oil, ginger and jalapeño. Set aside 2 tsp (10 mL) of mixture. Place salmon steaks in a dish just large enough to hold them. Pour remaining lime juice mixture over salmon and turn to coat. Marinate at room temperature for 15 minutes, turning once.

Preheat barbecue to medium-high and grease grill. Barbecue salmon, turning once, until cooked through, about 3 to 4 minutes per side. Remove to a platter and spoon reserved lime juice mixture over salmon. Serve immediately.

KITCHEN TIP: If you wish to broil salmon, place on a rack set over a pan. Broil about 4 inches (10 cm) from heat, turning once, until salmon is cooked through, about 3 to 4 minutes per side.

Salmon with Orange Balsamic Vinaigrette

This piquant sauce with a nice blend of fresh herbs pairs wonderfully with the richness of the salmon. Serve with steamed asparagus and wild rice or new potatoes.

4	salmon fillets (about 4 oz/125 g each), skin removed	4
Pinch	*each:* salt, freshly ground black pepper	Pinch
3 tsp	Becel margarine, divided	15 mL
¾ cup	orange juice	175 mL
¼ cup	balsamic vinegar	50 mL
2 tbsp	minced onion	30 mL
2 tsp	*each:* coarsely chopped fresh parsley, basil, mint	10 mL

Preparation: 15 minutes
Cooking Time: 7 to 10 minutes
Serves: 4

Preheat oven to 450°F (230°C). Season salmon with salt and pepper.

In a large nonstick skillet, melt 2 tsp (10 mL) of the margarine over medium-high heat. Place salmon in pan and cook for about 2 to 3 minutes on each side or until lightly browned. Transfer salmon to an oven-proof dish and roast for 5 to 7 minutes or until cooked through.

Wipe out skillet with a paper towel and stir in orange juice, balsamic vinegar and onion. Bring to a boil and boil 2 minutes or until sauce has thickened slightly. Remove from heat and stir in remaining 1 tsp (5 mL) margarine until melted. Stir in fresh herbs. Season to taste with pepper. Spoon sauce over salmon and serve immediately.

Nutrients per serving
Calories 226
Protein 22.9 g
Fat 10.1 g
   PUFA 4.1 g
   MUFA 3.6 g
   SFA 1.5 g
Carbohydrates 9.5 g
Fibre 0.3 g
Cholesterol 62 mg
Sodium 148 mg
Potassium 657 mg
Excellent source of riboflavin, niacin, vitamin B6, vitamin B12 and pantothenic acid.

Balsamic vinegar: Originating from the town of Modena in northern Italy, balsamic vinegar is made from unfermented grape juice that is aged in wooden casks. The quality of the vinegar depends a great deal on the type of wood used, the skill of the vinegar maker and the number of years it ages. It has a dark colour and a sweet pungent aroma and flavour. Balsamic vinegar is available at most major grocery stores.

Sole with Mixed Mushrooms en Papillote

A traditional French recipe brought up to date with the addition of specialty mixed mushrooms and fresh ginger. The green beans seasoned with garlic and thyme complement the fish nicely.

Preparation: 20 minutes
Baking Time: 15 minutes
Serves: 2

1 tbsp	Becel margarine	15 mL
1/2 lb	assorted mushrooms (shiitake, oyster and button), thinly sliced	250 g
2 tbsp	coarsely chopped fresh parsley	30 mL
1/2 tsp	grated lime or lemon rind	2 mL
1 tbsp	lime or lemon juice	15 mL
2 tsp	minced fresh ginger (or 3/4 tsp/3 mL ground ginger)	10 mL
2	sole fillets (about 1/2 lb/250 g)	2
	Salt and freshly ground black pepper to taste	
1/2 lb	tender green beans, trimmed	250 g
1 tbsp	Becel light margarine	15 mL
1	small clove garlic, minced	1
1/2 tsp	dried thyme (or 1 tsp/5 mL chopped fresh)	2 mL

Nutrients per serving
Calories 241
Protein 25.3 g
Fat 10.1 g
  PUFA 3.9 g
  MUFA 3.6 g
  SFA 1.5 g
Carbohydrates 14.1 g
Fibre 4.5 g
Cholesterol 54 mg
Sodium 189 mg
Potassium 1041 mg
Excellent source of
  riboflavin, niacin,
  folacin, vitamin B12,
  pantothenic acid,
  magnesium and iron.
Contains a high amount
  of dietary fibre.

Preheat oven to 400°F (200°C).

In a nonstick skillet over medium heat, melt margarine. Sauté mushrooms, stirring, until softened. Add parsley, lime rind, lime juice and ginger; sauté until mushrooms are lightly browned, about 5 minutes. Remove from heat.

On a large sheet of foil or parchment paper, place 1 sole fillet; season lightly with salt and pepper. Divide mushroom mixture in half. Spoon half of the mushroom mixture onto the sole fillet. Wrap foil securely to form a parcel. Repeat with the other fillet. Place on baking sheet and bake for 15 minutes.

Meanwhile, cook green beans in lightly salted boiling water until just tender. Drain well. In the same saucepan, melt margarine over medium heat. Add garlic and thyme; cook, stirring, 1 minute. Toss in beans and heat through. Season with salt and pepper.

To serve, place unopened package on plate with green beans.

Kitchen Tip: After securing the parcels, unwrap a small section, insert a straw, blow to inflate parcel, seal quickly and immediately bake. The hot air will cook the fish quickly and keep it moist.

Grilled Swordfish with Low-Fat Dill Sauce

Firm fish such as swordfish, shark or tuna steaks are ideal for this recipe. Do not let fish marinate too long or the acid in the marinade starts to "cook" it. Enjoy barbecued, grilled or broiled fish with a dollop of tangy Dill Sauce and garnish with dill sprigs.

Preparation: 15 minutes (including sauce)
Cooking Time: 10 minutes
Marinating Time: 1 hour
Serves: 4

1/3 cup	Becel oil	75 mL
1/3 cup	lime juice	75 mL
1 tbsp	coarsely ground black pepper	15 mL
1 tsp	paprika	5 mL
4	swordfish steaks (about 6 oz/175 g each)	4
DILL SAUCE		
1/2 cup	low-fat mayonnaise	125 mL
1/3 cup	light sour cream (5% MF)	75 mL
2 tsp	lime juice	10 mL
2 tsp	Dijon mustard	10 mL
2 tbsp	finely chopped fresh dill	30 mL

Nutrients per serving
Calories 309
Protein 35.3 g
Fat 12.8 g
  PUFA 3.8 g
  MUFA 5.2 g
  SFA 3.0 g
Carbohydrates 11.6 g
Fibre 0.1 g
Cholesterol 70 mg
Sodium 473 mg
Potassium 560 mg
Excellent source of niacin, vitamin B6 and vitamin B12.

In a glass or other non-metallic dish large enough to fit fish in 1 layer, mix together oil, lime juice, pepper and paprika.

Rinse fish with cold water and pat dry with paper towel; place in dish, turning to coat well with marinade. Refrigerate, covered, for 1 hour.

Meanwhile, prepare Dill Sauce: In a small bowl, whisk together mayonnaise, sour cream, lime juice, mustard and dill. Cover and refrigerate until ready to use.

Remove fish from marinade. To barbecue: Cook for 4 to 5 minutes per side or until flesh turns opaque. To broil: Cook under preheated broiler about 6 inches (15 cm) from element, 4 to 5 minutes per side or until flesh turns opaque. To grill: Cook on lightly oiled grill pan 4 to 5 minutes per side or until flesh turns opaque. Serve immediately with Dill Sauce on the side.

TIME SAVER: Cut fish into large cubes and thread on skewers with pieces of sweet pepper. Cook, turning often, about 5 minutes total.

Shrimp Risotto

This quick and easy recipe uses long-grain rice instead of Arborio (Italian short-grain rice).

2 tbsp	Becel margarine, divided	30 mL
3/4 lb	medium shrimp, peeled and deveined	375 g
2	cloves garlic, minced; divided	2
1 cup	slivered sweet red pepper	250 mL
1 cup	slivered sweet green pepper	250 mL
1	medium onion, chopped	1
1 cup	long-grain rice	250 mL
1/3 cup	dry white wine	75 mL
2 1/4 cups	water*	300 mL
1	packet sodium-reduced chicken bouillon*	1
1/4 tsp	freshly ground black pepper	1 mL
1/4 cup	*each:* grated Parmesan cheese, chopped fresh parsley	50 mL

* Or use 2 1/4 cups low-sodium chicken broth instead of water and bouillon

Preparation: 15 minutes
Cooking Time: 25 to 30 minutes
Serves: 4

In a large nonstick saucepan, melt 1 tbsp (15 mL) of the margarine over medium-high heat. Add shrimp and half of the garlic. Cook, stirring, for 2 to 3 minutes or until shrimp turns pink. Remove shrimp from pan.

Add peppers and cook 2 minutes; remove from pan.

Melt remaining margarine in pan. Cook remaining garlic and onion, stirring, for 5 minutes or until soft. Add rice; cook, stirring, 1 minute. Add wine; stir until most has been absorbed. Stir in water and packet chicken bouillon (or chicken broth) and pepper. Bring to a boil, stirring often. Cover and simmer over low heat 20 minutes or until rice is tender. The rice should be creamy, so don't overcook.)

Stir in Parmesan cheese and parsley, return shrimp and peppers to pan; mix and heat through. Serve immediately.

VARIATION: This is great for leftover cooked turkey or chicken. Omit shrimp. Add 2 cups (500 mL) diced cooked turkey or chicken with peppers at end of cooking time. Heat through.

Nutrients per serving
Calories 344
Protein 20 g
Fat 9 g
  PUFA 2.9 g
  MUFA 3.1 g
  SFA 2.3 g
Carbohydrates 42.9 g
Fibre 1.8 g
Cholesterol 102 mg
Sodium 433 mg
Potassium 298 mg
Excellent source of vitamin C, niacin, vitamin B12.

Lightly Seasoned Baked Fish Fingers

Serve this lighter alternative to deep-fried fish with green beans and a tomato salad.

Preparation: 10 minutes
Cooking Time: 10 minutes
Serves: 4

1 tbsp	Becel margarine, melted	15 mL
4	fresh or frozen and defrosted sole fillets	4
1/2 cup	all-purpose flour	125 mL
2	egg whites	2
3/4 cup	dried breadcrumbs	175 mL
1 tbsp	chopped fresh parsley (or if fresh parsley is unavailable use 1 tsp/5 mL dried basil)	15 mL
1 tsp	dried thyme (or 1 tbsp/15 mL chopped fresh)	5 mL
1/4 tsp	*each:* salt, freshly ground black pepper	1 mL
1	lemon, cut into wedges	1

Nutrients per serving
Calories 267
Protein 27.1 g
Fat 5.5 g
  PUFA 2.0 g
  MUFA 1.8 g
  SFA 1.0 g
Carbohydrates 25.8 g
Fibre 1.1 g
Cholesterol 55 mg
Sodium 441 mg
Potassium 507 mg
Excellent source of niacin and vitamin B12.

Preheat oven to 450°F (230°C). Grease a 13- x 9-inch (3.5-L) baking dish with melted margarine. Pat fish dry with paper towels. Cut fillets into thick finger-shaped pieces.

Place flour in a shallow baking dish. Beat egg whites in another shallow dish. In a third bowl, combine breadcrumbs, parsley, thyme, salt and pepper.

Dredge each piece of fish in flour, shaking off excess. Dip into egg whites; allow excess to drain off. Dip into herbed crumb mixture.

Place fish in prepared baking dish. Bake for 3 minutes. Turn and bake for another 2 to 3 minutes or until fish flakes easily with a fork. Serve fish with lemon wedges.

KITCHEN TIP: A good rule of thumb for cooking fish is 10 minutes in a 450°F (230°C) oven per inch (2.5 cm) of thickness for fresh fish, and 20 minutes for frozen fish.

Cajun Fish Fillets

This is a quick and flavourful way to prepare fish. This rub works equally well with salmon, swordfish, sea bass or tuna.

1 tbsp	paprika	15 mL
3/4 tsp	garlic powder	4 mL
1 tsp	dried thyme (or 1 tbsp/15 mL chopped fresh)	5 mL
1/4 tsp	*each:* salt, freshly ground black pepper	1 mL
Pinch	cayenne pepper	Pinch
2 tsp	Becel oil	10 mL
2	halibut fillets	250 g
	Lemon wedges	

Preparation: 5 minutes
Cooking Time: about 10 minutes
Serves: 2

In a small bowl, combine paprika, garlic powder, thyme, salt, black pepper, cayenne and oil to make a paste. Pat fish dry with paper towels. Using the back of a spoon, rub paste mixture evenly over the entire surface of the fish.

Preheat barbecue to medium-high and grease grill. Barbecue halibut, turning once, until cooked through, about 3 to 5 minutes per side. (Alternatively, you may cook fish in a nonstick skillet over medium-high heat.) Cooking time may vary depending on thickness of fish. Remove fish to a serving plate and serve with lemon wedges.

MAKE AHEAD TIP: Rub seasoning paste over fish, cover with plastic wrap and refrigerate for up to 2 hours before cooking.

Nutrients per serving:
Calories 150
Protein 21 g
Fat 5.8 g
 PUFA 2.6 g
 MUFA 2.2 g
 SFA 0.6 g
Carbohydrates 3.3 g
Fibre 0.9 g
Cholesterol 49 mg
Sodium 357 mg
Potassium 319 mg
Excellent source of niacin
 and vitamin B12.

Vegetables and Side Dishes

Fast

When You Have More Time

Maple Ginger Glazed Carrots

Here's an easy and intriguing alternative to steamed carrots. A nice accompaniment to grilled meats.

6	medium carrots	6
1 tbsp	Becel light margarine	15 mL
2 tbsp	pure maple syrup	30 mL
2 tsp	minced fresh ginger	10 mL

Preparation: 10 minutes
Cooking Time: 7 to 8 minutes
Serves: 4 to 6

Peel carrots and slice ¼ inch (5 mm) thick on the diagonal.

In a medium saucepan, cover carrots with water and bring to a boil. Cook on medium-high heat until carrots are tender, about 7 minutes. Drain well.

In same saucepan on medium heat, toss carrots with margarine, maple syrup and ginger. Serve immediately.

TIME SAVER TIP: Use packaged baby peeled carrots. Cook 10 to 12 minutes or until tender.

Nutrients per serving
Calories 88
Protein 1.3 g
Fat 1.6 g
   PUFA 0.6 g
   MUFA 0.6 g
   SFA 0.2 g
Carbohydrates 18.2 g
Fibre 3 g
Cholesterol 0 mg
Sodium 96 mg
Potassium 280 mg
Excellent source of
   vitamin A.

Spicy Sesame Green Beans

These beans, dressed with warm sesame oil and soy sauce, are tangy and full of flavour. If you don't like spicy food, either cut down on the hot pepper flakes or don't use any at all.

Preparation: 10 minutes
Cooking Time: 8 minutes
Serves: 4

1/2 lb	tender green beans, trimmed	250 g
1 tsp	Becel light margarine	5 mL
2	cloves garlic, minced	2
1 tsp	light soy sauce	5 mL
1/4 tsp	hot pepper flakes	1 mL
1/4 tsp	sesame oil	1 mL

Nutrients per serving
Calories 27
Protein 1.1 g
Fat 0.9 g
  PUFA 0.4 g
  MUFA 0.3 g
  SFA 0.1 g
Carbohydrates 4.5 g
Fibre 1.2 g
Cholesterol 0 mg
Sodium 58 mg
Potassium 158 mg

In a medium saucepan, cook green beans in boiling water until tender crisp, about 6 minutes. Drain.

Meanwhile, in a large skillet over medium-low heat, melt margarine. Sauté garlic about 2 minutes. Do not allow garlic to burn. Add beans, soy sauce, hot pepper flakes and sesame oil. Toss well to fully coat beans. Serve immediately.

> **Sesame oil** has a delicious nutty flavour and aroma. Make sure you choose the dark-coloured sesame oil made from toasted sesame seeds, as it has more flavour than the pale variety. Sesame oil is not generally used for cooking, but small amounts are added to foods to give them a delicate sesame flavour.

Opposite: Curried Cakes with Chutney Sauce (page 11.
Overleaf: Fresh Fruit Salad with Cranberry Dressing (page 6(

Corn with Lemon and Thyme

A quick and tasty way to dress up corn!

1 tbsp	Becel light margarine	15 mL
3 cups	frozen corn niblets	750 mL
1¹/₂ tsp	granulated sugar	7 mL
¹/₂ tsp	dried thyme (or 1¹/₂ tsp/7 mL chopped fresh)	2 mL
1¹/₂ tbsp	lemon juice	20 mL
	Salt and freshly ground black pepper to taste	

Preparation: 5 minutes
Cooking Time: 7 minutes
Serves: 4

In a large skillet over medium-high heat, melt margarine. Add corn, sugar and thyme. Cook, stirring occasionally until corn is tender, about 5 minutes. Stir in lemon juice and season with salt and pepper. Serve immediately.

Nutrients per serving
Calories 116
Protein 3.6 g
Fat 1.5 g
   PUFA 0.6 g
   MUFA 0.6 g
   SFA 0.2 g
Carbohydrates 26.4 g
Fibre 2.6 g
Cholesterol 0 mg
Sodium 28 mg
Potassium 175 mg
Contains a moderate
   amount of dietary fibre.

verleaf: Fudgy Low-fat Brownies (page 149)
pposite: Poached Pears with Caramel Sauce (page 150)

Parsnip and Pear Purée

Pears make a great flavour addition to parsnips. This dish is also wonderfully easy to make, since the parsnips and pears cook together. Especially good with roast chicken, turkey or pork.

Preparation: 10 minutes
Cooking Time: 15 to 20
  minutes
Serves: 4 to 6

1 lb	parsnips, peeled and cut into 3/4-inch (2-cm) chunks	500 g
3	firm Bartlett pears, peeled, cored and cubed	3
1 tbsp	Becel margarine	15 mL
1/4 tsp	*each:* ground nutmeg, ground ginger	1 mL
	Salt and freshly ground black pepper to taste	

Place parsnips and pears in a saucepan and cover with water. Cover and bring to a boil. Cook 15 to 20 minutes or until tender. Drain well.

Mash and stir in margarine, nutmeg, ginger, salt and pepper. Serve immediately.

Nutrients per serving
Calories 171
Protein 1.8 g
Fat 3.6 g
  PUFA 1.3 g
  MUFA 1.5 g
  SFA 0.5 g
Carbohydrates 35.9 g
Fibre 5.4 g
Cholesterol 0 mg
Sodium 179 mg
Potassium 491 mg
Excellent source of folacin.
  Contains a high amount
  of dietary fibre.

Bulgur Pilaf with Dried Cranberries

Here is an interesting change from rice. Bulgur is parboiled cracked wheat that is easy to prepare and has a nutty flavour and pleasant chewy texture. The dried cranberries provide a sweet/tart dimension.

2 tsp	Becel margarine, regular or salt free	10 mL
1	small onion, chopped	1
1/2 cup	chopped celery	125 mL
1 3/4 cups	chicken broth	425 mL
1 cup	bulgur	250 mL
1/2 cup	dried cranberries	125 mL
1/2 tsp	grated lemon rind	2 mL
1/2 tsp	dried oregano (or 1 1/2 tsp/7 mL chopped fresh)	2 mL
1/4 tsp	freshly ground black pepper	1 mL

Preparation: 10 minutes
Cooking Time: 15 to 20 minutes
Serves: 6

In a medium saucepan, heat margarine over medium heat. Sauté onion and celery 5 minutes. Stir in remaining ingredients. Cover and bring to a boil. Reduce heat to low and simmer 10 to 15 minutes or until bulgur is tender and liquid is absorbed.

KITCHEN TIP: Look for bulgur in the bulk section of supermarkets or in health food stores. Do not overcook or it will become dry and soft. Since bulgur contains wheat germ, it can turn rancid; store in an airtight container in the refrigerator or freezer.

SERVING SUGGESTION: Serve with grilled chicken breasts or pork chops and a salad.

SUBSTITUTION: Instead of dried cranberries, use other dried fruit such as apricots, raisins or cherries.

Nutrients per serving
Calories 134
Protein 4.5 g
Fat 1.9 g
  PUFA 0.7 g
  MUFA 0.7 g
  SFA 0.3 g
Carbohydrates 26.1 g
Fibre 3.7 g
Cholesterol 0 mg
Sodium 251 mg
Potassium 184 mg

Ginger Carrots and Broccoli with Sesame Seeds

This simple and colourful side dish features baby carrots and broccoli. Most supermarkets now carry packaged cleaned baby carrots in the produce section—they will save you a lot of time cutting and peeling.

Preparation: 10 minutes
Cooking Time: 10 minutes
Serves: 6

1	pkg (12 oz/349 g) peeled baby carrots	1
2 cups	broccoli florets	500 mL
1 tbsp	Becel margarine, regular or salt free	15 mL
1/2 cup	diagonally sliced celery	125 mL
1/4 cup	chopped sweet red pepper	50 mL
1 tbsp	sesame seeds	15 mL
2 tsp	minced fresh ginger	10 mL
	Salt and freshly ground black pepper to taste	

Nutrients per serving
Calories 57
Protein 1.6 g
Fat 2.8 g
  PUFA 1.2 g
  MUFA 1.1 g
  SFA 0.4 g
Carbohydrates 7.2 g
Fibre 2 g
Cholesterol 0 mg
Sodium 64 mg
Potassium 209 mg
Excellent source of
  vitamin A.

In a medium saucepan of boiling water, simmer carrots, partially covered, for 5 minutes. Add broccoli and continue cooking 3 minutes or until vegetables are tender. Drain well.

Meanwhile, in a large skillet, melt margarine over medium heat. Sauté celery, red pepper, sesame seeds and ginger 3 minutes or until tender.

Add carrots and broccoli to skillet and stir-fry until heated through. Season with salt and pepper.

SUBSTITUTION: Regular carrots may be used. Peel and slice into julienne sticks.

Lemon Roasted Potatoes

Instead of the usual roasted potatoes, these have less fat (and some might argue more flavour). If you can't find mini potatoes, cut regular potatoes into 1 1/2-inch (3-cm) chunks.

1 lb	mini potatoes, scrubbed and cut in half	500 g
1 tbsp	Becel margarine, melted	15 mL
1 tbsp	lemon juice	15 mL
1 tsp	finely grated lemon rind	5 mL
2 tbsp	finely chopped chives, parsley, basil or green onions	30 mL
	Salt and freshly ground black pepper to taste	

Preparation: 10 minutes
Cooking Time: 25 minutes
Serves: 4

Preheat oven to 425°F (220°C). Place potatoes in a medium saucepan and cover with cold water. Bring to a boil. Reduce heat and simmer until barely fork tender, about 3 minutes. Potatoes should still be quite hard (otherwise they will go mushy when you roast them).

Meanwhile, in a small bowl whisk together margarine and lemon juice. As soon as potatoes are cooked, drain well. Turn potatoes into a baking dish just large enough to hold them. Toss with lemon juice mixture. Bake, stirring occasionally, until golden and cooked through, 15 to 20 minutes.

Sprinkle with lemon rind, herbs or green onions, salt and pepper. Serve hot.

Nutrients per serving
Calories 107
Protein 1.9 g
Fat 2.8 g
　PUFA 1.2 g
　MUFA 1.1 g
　SFA 0.4 g
Carbohydrates 19.2 g
Fibre 1.7 g
Cholesterol 0 mg
Sodium 29 mg
Potassium 369 mg
Good source of vitamin B6.

Braised Fennel

Here's a perfect accompaniment to roast beef, pork or chicken. The nice thing is that there is no pan to clean up at the end. If you wish to barbecue, place foil packet over a medium-high heat on the grill. Barbecue for about 20 minutes, shaking package occasionally, until fennel is tender.

Preparation: 5 minutes
Baking Time: 20 minutes
Serves: 4

1	large fennel bulb	1
2 tsp	lemon juice	10 mL
1 tsp	Becel margarine	10 mL
	Salt and freshly ground black pepper to taste	
2 tbsp	water	30 mL

Nutrients per serving
Calories 31
Protein 0.9 g
Fat 1.1 g
   PUFA 0.4 g
   MUFA 0.4 g
   SFA 0.1 g
Carbohydrates 5.5 g
Fibre 2.3 g
Cholesterol 0 mg
Sodium 47 mg
Potassium 306 mg

Preheat oven to 375°F (190°C). Cut a large piece of heavy-duty foil measuring about 18 inches (45 cm) square.

Cut off any brownish parts of fennel and remove core. Cut bulb and stalks into 2-inch (5-cm) chunks. Place fennel in a bowl. Toss with lemon juice, then turn onto foil. Dot fennel with margarine. Sprinkle with salt, pepper and water. Seal foil to form a package.

Bake until fennel is tender but not mushy, shaking package occasionally to stir fennel, about 20 to 25 minutes. Serve hot.

Sautéed Spinach with Red Pepper

We're all looking for side dishes that are quick to prepare and healthy too. Here's a colourful one that fits the bill beautifully.

2	medium bunches fresh spinach	2
2 tsp	Becel margarine	10 mL
1/2	red pepper, finely diced	1/2
2	cloves garlic, minced	2
1/2 tsp	dried basil (or 1 1/2 tsp/7 mL chopped fresh)	2 mL
	Squeeze of lemon juice (optional)	
	Salt and freshly ground black pepper to taste	

Preparation: 5 minutes
Cooking Time: 4 minutes
Serves: 4

Remove any tough stems and very coarsely chop spinach. You should have about 12 cups (3 L). Wash spinach and shake off any excess water, but do not dry. Set aside.

In a large wide skillet, heat margarine over medium heat. Add red pepper, garlic and basil; cook, stirring frequently, just until red pepper softens slightly, about 2 minutes.

Increase heat to medium-high. Add spinach; cook, stirring frequently, just until spinach wilts, 2 to 3 minutes. Add a squeeze of lemon juice if you wish, and salt and pepper to taste. Serve hot.

TIME SAVER TIP: Use 1 pkg (10 oz/284 g) pre-washed spinach or baby spinach.

Nutrients per serving
Calories 60
Protein 5 g
Fat 2.3 g
 PUFA 0.9 g
 MUFA 0.8 g
 SFA 0.3 g
Carbohydrates 7.6 g
Fibre 4.6 g
Cholesterol 0 mg
Sodium 130 mg
Potassium 787 mg
Excellent source of vitamin A, vitamin C, folacin, magnesium and iron. Contains a high amount of dietary fibre.

Herbed Onion Potatoes

These potatoes feature the delectably tasty combination of parsley, sage, rosemary and thyme. Serve with roasted chicken, turkey or pork.

Preparation: 10 to 15 minutes
Cooking Time: 15 to 20 minutes
Serves: 4

2 lb	red potatoes (5 or 6 medium), unpeeled	1 kg
2 tbsp	Becel oil	30 mL
1¹/₂ cups	chopped red onion	375 mL
¹/₂ cup	diced sweet red pepper	125 mL
2	cloves garlic, minced	2
2 tsp	*each:* dried sage, rosemary, thyme	10 mL
	(or 1 tbsp/15 mL chopped fresh sage,	
	rosemary or thyme)	
¹/₄ cup	chopped fresh parsley	50 mL
	Salt and freshly ground black pepper to taste	

Nutrients per serving
Calories 250
Protein 4.7 g
Fat 6.9 g
  PUFA 3.1 g
  MUFA 3.0 g
  SFA 0.7 g
Carbohydrates 44.3 g
Fibre 4.4 g
Cholesterol 0 mg
Sodium 457 mg
Potassium 850 mg
Excellent source of vitamin
  C, vitamin B6. Contains a
  high amount of dietary
  fibre.

Cook potatoes in boiling salted water for 10 to 15 minutes or until slightly tender. Let cool. Cut into ³/₄-inch (2-cm) pieces.

In extra-large skillet or Dutch oven, heat oil over medium heat. Add onion, red pepper and garlic; sauté 2 minutes. Stir in potatoes and dried (or fresh) herbs. Cook, stirring often, for 10 to 15 minutes or until potatoes are fully cooked. Stir in parsley. Season to taste with salt and pepper; cook 30 seconds more. Serve hot.

Roasted Mixed Vegetables

Roasting vegetables gives them a wonderfully rich and intense flavour. Even finicky vegetable eaters will love these ones!

1 lb	unpeeled mini red or white potatoes	500 g
4	large carrots, peeled	4
2	medium onions, peeled	2
1/2 lb	cauliflower	250 g
2	cloves garlic, minced	2
2 tbsp	Becel oil	30 mL
2 tsp	dried basil (or 2 tbsp/30 mL chopped fresh)	10 mL
1/2 tsp	salt	2 mL
1/4 tsp	freshly ground black pepper	1 mL

Preparation: 15 minutes
Baking Time: 55 minutes
Serves: 6

Preheat oven to 425°F (220°C). Cut potatoes, carrots, onions and cauliflower into 1½-inch (4-cm) chunks. Place vegetables in 13- x 9-inch (3.5-L) baking pan.

Combine remaining ingredients. Pour over vegetables and toss to coat. Bake on middle rack of oven for 45 to 55 minutes, stirring occasionally, until vegetables are tender and browned.

SUBSTITUTIONS: Sweet potatoes, turnips, parsnips and broccoli are all high-fibre alternatives to the vegetables listed here.

Nutrients per serving
Calories 146
Protein 3.0 g
Fat 4.6 g
  PUFA 2.1 g
  MUFA 2.0 g
  SFA 0.4 g
Carbohydrates 24.5 g
Fibre 4.1 g
Cholesterol 0 mg
Sodium 239 mg
Potassium 533 mg
Excellent source of vitamin A, vitamin C and vitamin B6. Contains a high amount of dietary fibre.

Tropical Rice

To make this side dish even faster, look for quick-cooking brown rice. It's just as delicious and nutritious.

Preparation: 5 minutes
Cooking Time: 40 minutes
Serves: 4

2 cups	chicken broth, preferably sodium-reduced	500 mL
1 cup	brown rice	250 mL
1 tbsp	Becel RSF* or light margarine	15 mL
2 tbsp	raisins	30 mL
1	bay leaf	1

Nutrients per serving
Calories 206
Protein 4.5 g
Fat 2.7 g
   PUFA 0.9 g
   MUFA 0.9 g
   SFA 0.4 g
Carbohydrates 41.4 g
Fibre 2.5 g
Cholesterol 0 mg
Sodium 350 mg
Potassium 114 mg
Excellent source of
   magnesium.

In a medium saucepan, bring chicken broth to a boil. Add rice, margarine, raisins and bay leaf. Reduce heat, cover and simmer 25 to 40 minutes or until rice is tender and most of the water has been absorbed, depending on brown rice used. Remove from heat and let stand, covered, for 5 minutes. Remove bay leaf. Serve hot.

* See Appendix for details on Becel RSF.

Roasted Sweet Potatoes with Apples

Oven-roasted sweet potatoes with onions and apples are flavoured with rosemary in this great simple-to-prepare dish.

1 lb	sweet potatoes (2 or 3 medium), peeled and cut into 3/4-inch (2-cm) cubes	500 g
1	medium onion, peeled and cut into 8 wedges	1
1/4 cup	orange juice	50 mL
1 tbsp	packed brown sugar	15 mL
1/4 tsp	crumbled dried rosemary (or 3/4 tsp/3 mL chopped fresh)	1 mL
1/4 tsp	*each:* salt, freshly ground black pepper	1 mL
1 tbsp	Becel margarine, regular, salt free or light	15 mL
1	medium unpeeled Granny Smith apple, cored and sliced	1

Preparation: 10 minutes
Baking Time: 40 to 45 minutes
Serves: 6

Preheat oven to 350°F (180°C). In a greased 13- x 9-inch (3.5 L) baking pan, place sweet potatoes and onion.

Combine orange juice, sugar, rosemary, salt and pepper; pour over vegetables, stirring to coat. Dot with margarine.

Cover and bake 30 minutes, stirring occasionally. Add apples and bake, uncovered, 10 to 15 minutes longer or until apples and vegetables are tender. Serve hot.

SERVING SUGGESTION: Make a complete oven meal: serve with baked ham or pork or roast chicken. Add a green vegetable such as cooked broccoli and a salad to complete the meal.

Nutrients per serving
Calories 118
Protein 1.4 g
Fat 2.1 g
  PUFA 0.9 g
  MUFA 0.8 g
  SFA 0.3 g
Carbohydrates 24.2 g
Fibre 2.5 g
Cholesterol 0 mg
Sodium 122 mg
Potassium 198 mg
Excellent source of vitamin A.

Braised Red Cabbage

This tasty dish is sweetened with apples and a touch of brown sugar and soured with a bit of red wine vinegar. A great side dish with grilled sausages, pork or poultry.

Preparation: 20 minutes
Cooking Time: about 60 minutes
Serves: 4

2 tbsp	Becel oil	30 mL
1½ cups	thinly sliced red onion	375 mL
2	cloves garlic, minced	2
8 cups	thinly sliced red cabbage	2 L
3	apples, peeled if desired, cored and chopped	3
1 cup	chicken broth	250 mL
⅓ cup	red wine vinegar	75 mL
2 tbsp	light brown sugar	30 mL
2	bay leaves	2
	Salt and freshly ground black pepper to taste	

Nutrients per serving
Calories 202
Protein 3.6 g
Fat 7.5 g
 PUFA 3.3 g
 MUFA 3.1 g
 SFA 0.8 g
Carbohydrates 33.7 g
Fibre 6.3 g
Cholesterol 0 mg
Sodium 209 mg
Potassium 468 mg
Excellent source of vitamin C. Contains a very high amount of dietary fibre.

In a large saucepan or Dutch oven, heat oil over medium heat. Add onion and cook, stirring often, for 7 minutes or until softened. Stir in garlic, cabbage and apples. Cook, stirring often, until cabbage begins to wilt. Stir in chicken broth, vinegar, sugar and bay leaves. Reduce heat, cover and simmer for 45 minutes, stirring occasionally, or until cabbage is soft. Remove bay leaves. Season with salt and pepper. Serve hot.

VARIATIONS
- Add 1 tsp (5 mL) caraway seeds when you add the cabbage.
- Add ¼ cup (50 mL) red wine in place of the same amount of chicken broth.

Roasted Sweet Potatoes with Maple Syrup

Oven-roasting the sweet potato enhances its mellow flavour. Here its natural sweetness is nudged with a little maple syrup (after all, we are Canadian). This dish may be made ahead and reheated in the microwave or oven. Serve with roasted poultry or pork.

3 lb	sweet potatoes (about 4)	1.5 kg
1 tbsp	Becel margarine	15 mL
3 tbsp	maple syrup	45 mL
Pinch	ground nutmeg	Pinch

Preparation: 15 minutes
Cooking Time: 60 to 90 minutes
Serves: 6

Preheat oven to 400°F (200°C). Pierce sweet potatoes in several places to allow steam to escape. Place on a baking sheet. Bake for 60 to 70 minutes or until softened.

Let sweet potatoes cool slightly. Slice lengthwise and scoop out flesh into a medium bowl. Using a fork, mash together sweet potatoes and margarine until desired consistency. Stir in maple syrup and nutmeg. Spoon into casserole dish lightly greased with margarine. Smooth top and cover with lid or foil. Reheat in 375°F (190°C) for 20 to 30 minutes. (May be made ahead up to this point and refrigerated. Reheat in oven 10 minutes longer.) To reheat in microwave, microwave on High for about 5 minutes, stirring once, until heated through. (Turn once if you do not have a turntable.)

SUBSTITUTION: Substitute thawed frozen orange or apple juice concentrate for the maple syrup.

Nutrients per serving
Calories 208
Protein 2.8 g
Fat 2.0 g
  PUFA 0.8 g
  MUFA 0.8 g
  SFA 0.8 g
Carbohydrates 45.6 g
Fibre 4.9 g
Cholesterol 0 mg
Sodium 34 mg
Potassium 585 mg
Excellent source of vitamin A and vitamin C. Contains a high amount of dietary fibre.

Baking and Fruit Desserts

Fast

When You Have More Time

When baking or cooking with margarine, be sure to follow the recipe instructions. Since Becel light margarine contains half the fat (and therefore more moisture) of regular Becel margarine, it will perform differently in recipes and cooking applications. Replacing regular Becel with Becel light (or vice versa) will affect the quality of your baked goods. To ensure the best result, use the type of margarine called for in the recipe.

Baked Apples with Oatmeal Streusel

These baked apples have a wholesome filling of oats and dates.

4	large apples (McIntosh, Cortland or Empire)	4
¼ cup	quick-cooking rolled oats	50 mL
¼ cup	packed light brown sugar	50 mL
2 tbsp	finely chopped dates or dried apricots	30 mL
½ tsp	ground cinnamon	2 mL
2 tsp	Becel margarine, regular, light or salt free	10 mL
⅓ cup	unsweetened apple juice	75 mL

Preparation: 10 minutes
Baking Time: 35 to 45 minutes
Serves: 4

Preheat oven to 350°F (180°C).

Cut a 1¼-inch (3-cm) diameter core from centre of each apple, almost but not all the way through to bottom. Remove peel about one-third way down from top. Place apples in shallow 8-inch/ (20-cm) glass pie plate.

In a small bowl, combine oats, brown sugar, dates and cinnamon. Fill each apple with mixture, packing firmly (pat any remaining oat mixture on top of apples). Place ½ tsp (2 mL) margarine on top of filling in each apple. Pour apple juice into dish.

Bake apples, uncovered, for 35 to 45 minutes or until tender. Cool slightly before serving.

KITCHEN TIP
- Apples may also be cooked in the microwave: Cover baking dish with waxed paper. Microwave on 70% power for 6 to 8 minutes, turning and basting each apple halfway through cooking time, until apples are just tender.

Nutrients per serving
Calories 233
Protein 1.3 g
Fat 3 g
  PUFA 1.1 g
  MUFA 0.9 g
  SFA 0.5 g
Carbohydrates 54.5 g
Fibre 5.8 g
Cholesterol 0 mg
Sodium 22 mg
Potassium 340 mg
Contains a high amount of dietary fibre.

Blueberry Lemon Crunch

The sweetness of the blueberries contrasts beautifully with the crunch of the oatmeal.

Preparation: 10 minutes
Baking Time: 30 minutes
Serves: 6

3 cups	fresh or frozen blueberries	750 mL
1 cup	quick-cooking rolled oats	250 mL
1/2 cup	light brown sugar	125 mL
1/4 cup	Becel RSF margarine,* melted	50 mL
2 tbsp	all-purpose flour	30 mL
2 tsp	grated lemon rind	10 mL

Nutrients per serving
(calculated with RSF)
Calories 193
Protein 3.2 g
Fat 3.6 g
  PUFA 1.4 g
  MUFA 1.3 g
  SFA 0.5 g
Carbohydrates 38.9 g
Fibre 3.6 g
Cholesterol 0 mg
Sodium 58 mg
Potassium 180 mg
Contains a high amount of
  dietary fibre.

Preheat oven to 350°F (180°C).

Place blueberries in a small baking dish. Combine oats, brown sugar, margarine, flour and lemon rind until crumbly. Sprinkle mixture over fruit. Bake for about 30 minutes or until fruit is hot and topping is set. Serve warm.

* If Becel RSF is not available in your area, substitute the same amount of Becel light.

Seasonal Fruit Crisp

Easy to make and always a favourite. Use a combination of seasonal fresh fruits such as plums, pears or apples. Pop in the oven just before sitting down for dinner and this will be ready to serve once you've finished the main course.

FRUIT FILLING

2¹/2 cups	ripe purple plums, pitted and sliced	625 mL
2¹/2 cups	ripe pears, peeled, cored and sliced	625 mL
¹/2 cup	packed light brown sugar	125 mL
1 tbsp	cornstarch	15 mL
¹/4 tsp	*each:* ground nutmeg, ground ginger	1 mL

TOPPING

1 cup	quick-cooking rolled oats	250 mL
³/4 cup	all-purpose flour	175 mL
¹/2 cup	packed light brown sugar	125 mL
¹/3 cup	Becel light margarine, melted	75 mL

Preparation: 25 minutes
Baking Time: 40 minutes
Serves: 8

Preheat oven to 400°F (200°C). Spray an 11- x 7-inch (2-L) baking dish with nonstick cooking spray.

Toss sliced fruit with brown sugar, cornstarch, nutmeg and ginger. Spread fruit mixture evenly into prepared baking dish.

To make Topping: In a medium bowl, using a fork, toss together rolled oats, flour, brown sugar and melted margarine until combined. Sprinkle oat mixture evenly over fruit.

Bake for 30 to 40 minutes or until topping is golden brown and fruit is tender.

SUBSTITUTION: Use peeled, cored and sliced apples instead of plums; reduce sugar to ¹/3 cup (75 mL) in the filling.

Nutrients per serving
Calories 281
Protein 3.6 g
Fat 4.9 g
 PUFA 1.9 g
 MUFA 1.9 g
 SFA 0.6 g
Carbohydrates 57.7 g
Fibre 3.5 g
Cholesterol 0 mg
Sodium 66 mg
Potassium 289 mg
Good source of iron.
 Contains a moderate amount of dietary fibre.

Raspberry Pear Pudding

The aroma of this pudding while it's baking is simply divine! This recipe is adapted from a classic French custard flan called clafoutis, which is traditionally baked in a sweet pastry crust. We've removed the pastry for a lighter alternative. In summer, substitute frozen raspberries for fresh pitted cherries, blueberries or blackberries.

Preparation: 15 minutes
Baking Time: 20 to 23 minutes
Serves: 6

1 tbsp	Becel margarine	15 mL
1	ripe pear, peeled, cored and chopped	1
1 cup	fresh or frozen raspberries	250 mL
2 tbsp	all-purpose flour, divided	30 mL
2	eggs	2
1/3 cup	evaporated skim milk (or evaporated 2%)	75 mL
1/4 cup	granulated sugar	50 mL
1 tsp	vanilla	5 mL
1 tsp	icing sugar	5 mL

Nutrients per serving
Calories 155
Protein 3.6 g
Fat 3.7 g
  PUFA 1.0 g
  MUFA 1.4 g
  SFA 0.8 g
Carbohydrates 26.8 g
Fibre 1.2 g
Cholesterol 72 mg
Sodium 55 mg
Potassium 110 mg

Preheat oven to 400°F (200°C). Grease a 9-inch (23-cm) pie plate with margarine. In a bowl, toss pears and raspberries with 1 tbsp (15 mL) of the flour. Distribute fruit evenly in pie plate.

In a medium bowl, using a whisk, beat together eggs, evaporated skim milk, sugar, vanilla and remaining 1 tbsp (15 mL) flour until smooth. Pour the egg mixture over the fruit.

Bake for 20 to 23 minutes or until puffed and set. Cool on rack 10 minutes before serving. Dust with sifted icing sugar.

Mixed Fruit Cobbler

An easy and comforting dessert to enjoy any time. Vary the fruits in the recipe to suit the season.

¼ cup	granulated sugar	50 mL
2 tbsp	cornstarch	30 mL
1 tsp	ground cinnamon	5 mL
3	medium apples, cored and sliced	3
3	pears, cored and sliced	3
½ cup	dried apricots, slivered	125 mL
1 cup	orange juice	250 mL

TOPPING

¾ cup	all-purpose flour	175 mL
2 tbsp	granulated sugar	30 mL
¾ tsp	baking powder	4 mL
¼ tsp	baking soda	1 mL
¼ tsp	salt	1 mL
3 tbsp	Becel light margarine	45 mL
½ cup	low-fat plain yogurt (1% MF)	125 mL
1 tsp	grated orange rind	5 mL

Preparation: 25 minutes
Baking Time: 25 to 30 minutes
Serves: 8

Preheat oven to 400°F (200°C).

In a large bowl, combine sugar, cornstarch and cinnamon. Toss with apples, pears and apricots. Spoon into 2½-quart (2.5-L) or 9-inch (23-cm) square baking dish. Pour orange juice over top.

To prepare topping: In a large bowl, mix together flour, sugar, baking powder, baking soda and salt. Cut in margarine until mixture resembles coarse crumbs. Combine yogurt and orange rind. Stir into flour mixture until just moistened. Using a large spoon, drop into 8 mounds on top of fruit.

Bake 25 to 30 minutes or until golden brown and fruit is tender. Serve warm.

Nutrients per serving
Calories 216
Protein 2.9 g
Fat 2.8 g
  PUFA 1.0 g
  MUFA 0.9 g
  SFA 0.5 g
Carbohydrates 47.3 g
Fibre 4.3 g
Cholesterol 1 mg
Sodium 176 mg
Potassium 354 mg
Contains a high amount of dietary fibre.

Fruit Puffs

These delicate puffs are a nice way to end a special dinner. Fill the puffs just before serving, or they will become too soft.

Preparation: 10 minutes
Baking Time: 30 minutes
Makes 16 puffs

PUFFS

1 cup	water	250 mL
1/3 cup	Becel light margarine	75 mL
1 cup	all-purpose flour	250 mL
Pinch	salt	Pinch
4	eggs (or 3 whole eggs and 2 egg whites)	4

FILLING

4 cups	frozen yogurt or prepared light whipped topping	1 L
3 cups	(approx.) fresh fruit (sliced strawberries or peaches, raspberries, blueberries)	750 mL
1/2 cup	light jam (strawberry, raspberry, apricot) Icing sugar for garnish	125 mL

Nutrients per serving
(1 puff)
Calories 165
Protein 4.6 g
Fat 5.7 g
   PUFA 1.0 g
   MUFA 1.9 g
   SFA 2.3 g
Carbohydrates 23.8 g
Fibre 1 g
Cholesterol 58 mg
Sodium 72 mg
Potassium 133 mg
Good source of vitamin
   B12.

Preheat oven to 400°F (200°C).

Heat water and margarine in medium saucepan to a rolling boil. Add flour and salt all at once. Turn heat to low and stir vigorously about 2 minutes or until mixture leaves sides of pan and forms a ball. Remove from heat; cool 5 minutes.

Using medium speed of an electric mixer or beating vigorously with a wooden spoon, add eggs 1 at a time to flour mixture, mixing vigorously after each egg until smooth and glossy. Drop dough by heaping tablespoons 2 inches (5 cm) apart to a baking sheet.

Bake for 25 to 30 minutes or until balls are puffed and golden. Slit side of each puff with tip of a sharp knife to allow steam to escape. Bake 2 minutes more. Cool completely on rack.

Cut puffs in half horizontally. Spoon 1 1/2 tsp (7 mL) jam on bottom of each puff. Top with 1/4 cup (50 mL) frozen yogurt or whipped topping and 1/4 cup (50 mL) fruit. Place puff top over filling. Dust puffs lightly with a little icing sugar and serve immediately.

Fudgy Low-Fat Brownies

These rich, moist and intensely chocolatey brownies are surprisingly low in fat.

2 tbsp	Becel margarine	30 mL
1/2 cup	cocoa powder	125 mL
1 cup	granulated sugar	250 mL
1	egg	1
3/4 cup	unsweetened applesauce	175 mL
2 tsp	vanilla	10 mL
1/2 cup	all-purpose flour	125 mL
1/4 tsp	*each:* baking soda, salt	2 mL

Preparation: 15 minutes
Baking Time: 25 to 30 minutes
Makes 16 brownies

Preheat oven to 350°F (180°C). Spray an 8-inch (20-cm) square baking pan with nonstick cooking spray. Dust with cocoa, shaking out excess.

In a small saucepan, melt margarine on low heat. Remove from heat and stir in cocoa, sugar, egg, applesauce and vanilla, beating until smooth. Gently stir in flour, baking soda and salt until well combined.

Pour into prepared pan and bake 25 to 30 minutes or until set. Cool completely and cut into 16 squares with hot, wet knife. Store in the refrigerator.

SERVING SUGGESTION: Serve brownies with raspberry orange sauce (page 152).

Nutrients per brownie:
Calories 95
Protein 1.3 g
Fat 2.5 g
  PUFA 0.6 g
  MUFA 1.0 g
  SFA 0.7 g
Carbohydrates 18.2 g
Fibre 1.3 g
Cholesterol 13 mg
Sodium 92 mg
Potassium 36 mg

Poached Pears with Caramel Sauce

The pears and sauce for this elegant dessert may be prepared a day in advance; simply cover and refrigerate. Remaining poaching liquid may be refrigerated for a week and used to poach other fruit. Or add soda water to it and serve with ice for a refreshing drink. Poaching water may also be frozen. The caramel sauce is delicious over frozen vanilla yogurt, plain yogurt or angel or pound cake.

Preparation: 10 minutes
Poaching Time: 17 minutes
Cooking Time: 5 to 10 minutes
Serves: 2

1/2	lemon	1/2
2 cups	water	500 mL
1/2 cup	granulated sugar	125 mL
2	cinnamon sticks (each 3 inches/8 cm)	2
2	whole cloves	2
2	firm but ripe pears	2

Caramel Sauce

1/2 cup	granulated sugar	125 mL
1/4 cup	water	50 mL
1 tsp	freshly squeezed lemon juice	5 mL
2 tsp	Becel margarine	10 mL
1 tsp	vanilla	5 mL
	Low-fat plain yogurt (1% MF) and mint leaves for garnish (optional)	

Nutrients per serving
Calories 211
Protein .6 g
Fat 2.4 g
  PUFA 0.9 g
  MUFA 0.9 g
  SFA 0.3 g
Carbohydrates 49.5 g
Fibre 2.9 g
Cholesterol 0 mg
Sodium 17 mg
Potassium 166 mg

Remove three wide strips of rind from lemon, being careful not to remove any of the white part. Squeeze out 2 tbsp (30 mL) lemon juice. Place lemon rind and juice in a medium saucepan along with water, sugar, cinnamon sticks and cloves. Cover and bring to a boil; reduce heat and simmer 5 minutes.

Meanwhile, leaving pear whole and stem intact, peel fruit. Using a small spoon or melon baller, carefully remove core from underside of pears. Place pears in simmering water-spice mixture. Simmer, covered, turning pears occasionally, until pears are tender, about 8 to 12 minutes, depending on ripeness of pear. Transfer pears with a slotted spoon to a covered dish. Reserve poaching liquid.

To prepare Caramel Sauce, place sugar, water and lemon juice in a small saucepan. Set over medium heat, stirring just until sugar dissolves. Once sugar dissolves, stop stirring. Continue to cook mixture, swirling pan occasionally until it turns a deep caramel colour, about 5 minutes. Watch carefully to prevent burning and immediately remove from heat once caramel has reached a deep caramel colour. Stir in 3 tbsp (45 mL) of the poaching liquid, margarine and vanilla. Cool sauce to room temperature.

To serve, spoon a couple of tablespoons of the sauce onto a dessert plate. Place pear on top. Garnish with a dollop of yogurt and a sprig of mint, if you wish.

KITCHEN TIP: Recipe can serve 4; use 4 pears but do not change quantity of other ingredients.

Baked Cheesecake with Raspberry Orange Sauce

No one will be able to resist this smooth and creamy cheesecake. A perfect dessert for special occasions.

Preparation: 30 minutes
Baking Time: 50 to 60 minutes
Chilling Time: minimum 2 hours
Serves: 12

CRUST

1 cup	graham crumbs	250 mL
1 tbsp	Becel light margarine, melted	15 mL

FILLING

2 cups	low-fat cottage cheese (1% MF)	500 mL
1	pkg (250-g) light cream cheese	1
2/3 cup	granulated sugar	150 mL
1/2 cup	low-fat plain yogurt (1% MF)	125 mL
1/4 cup	all-purpose flour	50 mL
2	egg whites	2
1	egg	1
1 tbsp	grated orange rind	15 mL
1 tsp	vanilla	5 mL

TOPPING

2 cups	fresh or frozen raspberries	500 mL
1/2 cup	orange juice	125 mL
1/3 cup	granulated sugar	75 mL
1 tbsp	cornstarch	15 mL
2 tbsp	cold water	30 mL

Nutrients per serving
Calories 226
Protein 9.3 g
Fat 6.9 g
  PUFA 0.7 g
  MUFA 2.3 g
  SFA 3.5 g
Carbohydrates 32.4 g
Fibre 1.4 g
Cholesterol 38 mg
Sodium 347 mg
Potassium 191 mg

Preheat oven to 325°F (160°C).

Combine Crust ingredients. Press into bottom of 9-inch (23-cm) springform pan. Bake for 5 minutes. Remove crust from oven; leave oven on.

To make Filling: In a food processor, blend cottage cheese until smooth. Add cream cheese and process until smooth. Add sugar, yogurt, flour, egg whites, egg, orange rind and vanilla; process until smooth. Pour into pan. Bake for 50 to 60 minutes or until almost set in centre.

Run knife around edge of cake to loosen from rim. Cool on rack. Chill for at least 2 hours. (Don't worry if cheesecake cracks slightly—it will be covered with raspberry topping.)

To make Topping: Combine raspberries, orange juice and sugar in saucepan. Bring to a boil, stirring constantly. Dissolve cornstarch in water. Add to pan and cook, stirring, 2 minutes.

Chill topping until cold, about 15 minutes. Spread over cake before serving.

Strawberry Almond Shortcakes

These individual shortcakes are a great idea for a summertime afternoon tea when local strawberries are in abundance. You can also serve the shortcakes warm without the filling, spread with just a little Becel margarine and some fruit preserves.

Preparation: 20 minutes
Baking Time: 8 to 10 minutes
Makes 8 cakes

SHORTCAKES

1 cup	all-purpose flour	250 mL
1 cup	cake and pastry flour	250 mL
1/3 cup	granulated sugar	75 mL
1 tbsp	baking powder	15 mL
1/2 tsp	baking soda	2 mL
1/2 tsp	salt	2 mL
3 tbsp	Becel margarine	45 mL
2/3 cup	buttermilk or sour milk	150 mL
1/2 tsp	almond extract	2 mL

TOPPING

1 tsp	skim milk	5 mL
2 tbsp	slivered almonds	30 mL
1 tbsp	granulated sugar	15 mL

FILLING

2 cups	fresh strawberries, hulled and sliced	500 mL
2 cups	plain frozen yogurt	500 mL

Nutrients per serving
Calories 253
Protein 5.5 g
Fat 6.1 g
 PUFA 1.9 g
 MUFA 2.4 g
 SFA 1.4 g
Carbohydrates 44 g
Fibre 1.8 g
Cholesterol 3 mg
Sodium 377 mg
Potassium 203 mg
Good source of vitamin C, folacin and iron.

Preheat oven to 425°F (220°C). Lightly spray a baking sheet with nonstick cooking spray.

In a medium bowl, whisk together all-purpose flour, cake and pastry flour, sugar, baking powder, baking soda and salt. With a pastry blender cut in margarine until it resembles coarse meal.

In a small bowl, whisk together buttermilk and almond extract.

Make a well in the dry ingredients. Add wet ingredients and stir with a fork until well combined. (Dough will be slightly sticky; do not overmix.)

Baking and Fruit Desserts

Turn dough onto a lightly floured surface. Gradually roll to about $\frac{1}{2}$-inch (1-cm) thickness. With a floured 3-inch (8-cm) cutter, cut out 8 shortcakes and place on prepared baking sheet. Brush shortcake tops with a little skim milk and sprinkle with slivered almonds and granulated sugar. Bake for 8 to 10 minutes or until light golden.

To serve, split shortcakes in half with a serrated knife. Place bottoms on dessert plates. Spoon on fresh strawberries and $\frac{1}{4}$ cup (50 mL) frozen yogurt per shortcake. Set tops on an angle. Serve immediately.

SUBSTITUTIONS: Substitute sliced peeled fresh peaches or raspberries for the strawberries.

Apricot Almond Biscotti

Biscotti are twice-baked Italian cookies that are perfect for dunking in a cup of tea or frothy latte.

Preparation: about 45 minutes
Baking Time: 50 minutes
Makes 36 biscotti

3 cups	all-purpose flour	750 mL
1 cup	granulated sugar	250 mL
3/4 tsp	baking soda	4 mL
1/4 tsp	salt	1 mL
1/2 cup	finely chopped dried apricots	125 mL
1/3 cup	slivered toasted almonds	75 mL
2	eggs	2
2	egg whites	2
3 tbsp	Becel margarine, melted	45 mL
1 tsp	almond extract	5 mL

Nutrients per serving
Calories 84
Protein 1.9 g
Fat 1.8 g
  PUFA 0.6 g
  MUFA 0.8 g
  SFA 0.3 g
Carbohydrates 14.9 g
Fibre 0.6 g
Cholesterol 12 mg
Sodium 56 mg
Potassium 51 mg

Preheat oven to 350°F (180°C).

In a large bowl, stir together flour, sugar, baking soda, salt, apricots and almonds. Make a well in centre of flour mixture.

Drop in eggs, egg whites, margarine and almond extract; whisk until blended. Stir in dry ingredients until combined.

Form dough into a ball. Place on a baking sheet. With slightly wet hands, form dough into a 16-inch (40-cm) long log. Flatten log to 1-inch (2.5-cm) thickness. Bake until light brown and cracked on top, about 30 minutes. Cool log on baking sheet for 10 minutes. Reduce oven temperature to 325°F (160°C).

Place warm log on cutting board. Using a serrated knife, cut log on sharp diagonal into 1/3-inch (8-mm) slices. Arrange on baking sheet. Bake 20 to 25 minutes or until pale golden brown. Cool biscotti on baking sheet (biscotti will harden while cooling). Store biscotti in an airtight container to maintain crispness.

SUBSTITUTION: Substitute golden raisins or dried cranberries for the apricots.

Toasted Almonds
Place almonds on a baking sheet and bake in a preheated 350°F (180°C) oven, stirring occasionally, for 5 to 7 minutes or until golden.

Applesauce Date Muffins

These fabulous muffins are packed with fibre. They're terrific as part of a healthy breakfast or a nutritious snack.

²/₃ cup	bran cereal (not flakes)	150 mL
1³/₄ cups	unsweetened applesauce	425 mL
1	egg, lightly beaten	1
³/₄ cup	chopped dates	175 mL
¹/₃ cup	packed light brown sugar	75 mL
3 tbsp	Becel margarine, melted	45 mL
1¹/₂ cups	whole wheat flour	375 mL
1 tsp	baking soda	5 mL
¹/₂ tsp	*each:* ground cinnamon, salt	2 mL

Preparation: 15 minutes
Baking Time: 25 minutes
Makes 12 muffins

Preheat oven to 375°F (190°C). Spray muffin tins with nonstick cooking spray.

In a medium bowl, combine bran cereal and applesauce; let stand 5 minutes. Stir in egg, dates, brown sugar and margarine.

In a large bowl, blend flour, baking soda, cinnamon and salt. Stir cereal mixture into dry ingredients until just moistened.

Spoon batter into muffin cups. Bake for 25 minutes or until set and golden. Cool on rack.

Nutrients per muffin
Calories 159
Protein 3.3 g
Fat 3.6 g
    PUFA 1.3 g
    MUFA 1.3 g
    SFA 0.6 g
Carbohydrates 31.8 g
Fibre 4.6 g
Cholesterol 18 mg
Sodium 259 mg
Potassium 225 mg
Good source of magnesium.
    Contains a high amount
    of dietary fibre.

Cranberry Orange Muffins

Moist and flavourful muffins with cranberries, oranges and the wholesomeness of bran. Be sure to have cranberries in your freezer to prepare these muffins any time.

Preparation: 15 minutes
Baking Time: 25 minutes
Makes 12 large muffins

1¼ cups	bran cereal (not flakes)	300 mL
1⅓ cups	low-fat plain yogurt (0.1% MF)	325 mL
1	egg, lightly beaten	1
½ cup	orange juice	125 mL
½ cup	liquid honey	125 mL
¼ cup	Becel margarine, melted	50 mL
1 tbsp	grated orange rind	15 mL
1 cup	all-purpose flour	250 mL
1 cup	whole wheat flour	250 mL
2 tsp	baking powder	10 mL
½ tsp	baking soda	2 mL
½ tsp	salt	2 mL
1 cup	fresh or frozen cranberries, coarsely chopped	250 mL

Nutrients per muffin
Calories 193
Protein 5.3 g
Fat 4.5 g
  PUFA 1.7 g
  MUFA 1.7 g
  SFA 0.7 g
Carbohydrates 36.2 g
Fibre 4.2 g
Cholesterol 18 mg
Sodium 307 mg
Potassium 228 mg
Good source of thiamine, magnesium and iron. Contains a high amount of dietary fibre.

Preheat oven to 375°F (190°C). Spray muffin tins with nonstick cooking spray.

Combine cereal and yogurt in mixing bowl; let stand 5 minutes. Stir in egg, orange juice, honey, melted margarine and orange rind. Mix well.

In a large bowl, combine all-purpose flour, whole wheat flour, baking powder, baking soda and salt. Stir cereal mixture and cranberries into dry mixture until just combined.

Fill greased muffin cups with batter. Bake 25 minutes or until set and golden. Cool on rack. Store in airtight container or freeze.

SUBSTITUTION: Substitute fresh or frozen blueberries for cranberries.

Index